12-7

A MESSAGE
TO THE CHARNWOOD READER
FROM THE PUBLISHER

Since the introduction of Ulverscroft Large Print Books, countless readers around the world have confirmed that the larger and clearer print has brought back the pleasure of reading to an ever-widening audience, thus enabling readers to once again enjoy the companionship of books which had previously been denied to them due to their inability to read normal small print.

It is obvious that to cater for this ever-widening audience of readers a new series was necessary. The Charnwood Series embraces the widest possible variety of literature from the traditional classics to the most recently published bestsellers, and includes many authors considered too contemporary both in subject and style to be suitable for the many elderly readers for whom the original Ulverscroft Large Print Books were designed.

The newly developed typeface of the Charnwood Series has been subjected to extensive and exhaustive tests amongst the international family of large print readers, and unanimously acclaimed and preferred as a smoother and easier read. Another benefit of this new typeface is that it allows the publication in one volume of longer novels which previously could only be published in two large print volumes: a constant source of frustration for readers when one volume is not available for one reason or another.

The Charnwood Series is designed to increase the titles available to those readers in this ever-widening audience who are unable to read and enjoy the range of popular titles at present only available in normal small print.

PRINCESS ANNE

The many faces of Princess Anne are revealed in this thoroughly researched biography of a princess for today's world. The respect and affection in which Princess Anne is held was not won easily. Finding a role that was worthy of this intelligent, forthright and compassionate woman involved being a success in several different spheres. Princess Anne has refused to sit back in comfort, and instead has striven and succeeded in finding a unique place for herself in the Royal Family and in the Britain of the 1980s.

NICHOLAS COURTNEY

PRINCESS ANNE
A Biography

Complete and Unabridged

CHARNWOOD
Leicester

First published in Great Britain in 1986 by
George Weidenfeld & Nicolson Ltd.,
London

First Charnwood Edition
published June 1987
by arrangement with
George Weidenfeld & Nicolson Ltd.,
London

British Library CIP Data

Courtney, Nicholas
    Princess Anne: a biography.—Large print ed.—
Charnwood library series
    1. Anne, *Princess, daughter of Elizabeth II,*
Queen of Great Britain   2. Great Britain—
Princes and princesses—Biography
    I. Title
    941.085'092'4   PA591.A34

    ISBN 0-7089-8409-6

Published by
F. A. Thorpe (Publishing) Ltd.
Anstey, Leicestershire
Set by Rowland Phototypesetting Ltd.
Bury St. Edmunds, Suffolk
Printed and bound in Great Britain by
T. J. Press (Padstow) Ltd., Padstow, Cornwall

For Vanessa

List of Illustrations

Acknowledgements

I FIRST ackowledge my gratitude to Lt.-Col. Peter Gibbs, Private Secretary to HRH The Princess Anne, and to Mr. John Haslan, her Press Secretary, for reading this biography and for their comments on the text.

In the editing of this biography, my editor (quite rightly) removed the source notes that peppered the text. Notwithstanding that loss, I would like to acknowledge and thank collectively those on whom I have drawn for information, especially Brian Hoey author of the excellent *HRH The Princess Anne, A Biography* (1984); Kenneth Harris's interview in the *Observer* (30 August 1980); Genevieve Murphy *Princess Anne and Mark Phillips, Talking about Horses* (1976); Jeffrey Barnard; Angela Rippon *Mark Phillips, the Man and his Horses* (1982); the 14th/20th King's Hussars Magazine; the Auberon Waugh Diaries; John Pearson *The Ultimate Family*; Georgina Howell for her interview in *The Sunday Times* (4 August 1985).

I would like to thank, again collectively, those who made this biography even more enjoyable to write by enthusing about my subject to a willing listener.

ILLUSTRATION ACKNOWLEDGEMENTS

The photographs in this book are reproduced by kind permission of Syndication International; British Railways Board 23 below; Michael Charity 24 above.

Prologue

THERE is no mistaking the horse-box. It is vast, pale blue, with dark-blue stripes down the side and the legend "Range Rover Team" across the back. It travels sedately, gliding round the bends of the narrow country lane like a gentle whale. No one takes much notice of it, not even the extra police drafted in for the week-end who pad up and down the verges in their big, black Wellington boots and heavy coats. Finally, it takes a wide sweep and eases through the narrow gateposts, over the cattle grid with a sound like a burst of machine-gun fire, then down towards the stables of the big house below.

The horse-box stops and a girl groom jumps out to open the heavy iron gates into the stable-yard. Inch by inch the box is edged through the archway with no more than hand's-breadth to spare on either side and at the top. Finally, it stops by the mounting block and the driver jumps to the ground, cap pulled low over her eyes. The cap is of black corduroy, in a style once made fashionable by the racing driver

Jackie Stewart. From the passenger side, another groom appears, followed by a man in a tweed coat; a brindle lurcher, Laura, bounds after him. They have all been there many times before and know the form. The driver looks at each horse— there are four of them—to make sure they have travelled well, before they are led off into the stables. Then the driver makes her way to the house, entering by the back door. She walks through the kitchens, nods to the two cooks she met the year before, then on through the green baize door to the hall. For the first time since her arrival, the driver is recognised as HRH The Princess Anne, Mrs. Mark Phillips. The police are embarrassed that they have missed her, although they need not have worried as her detective is with her.

Her hostess rushes out of the dining-room to meet her. She drops a shallow curtsey, welcomes her to her house, then rushes back to the dining room—one of the pekinese has been sick on the carpet. Princess Anne is treated as just another guest in the house-party come to stay for the week-end and compete in the horse trials in the park. She chats to her many friends from the eventing world among the milling crowd in the hall. They are completely at ease with her, (their initial curtseys and neck-bows are involuntary). They call her Ma'am; it rhymes with Anne.

With a swirl of gravel outside, Mark Phillips arrives, all teeth and smiles. He carries their suitcases himself up to their usual room, before catching up on the news over a mug of tea in the horse trials office. They scrutinise the programme, taking in their fellow competitors, their horses and the map of the course. It is an important horse trials for them: as it is considered the warm-up for Badminton, the top names in eventing are all there. Then, with a few friends, Princess Anne and Mark Phillips walk the course. Some of the fences are new. In the fading light, they discuss the take-offs and the landings, the angles and the problems. They talk about their horses and their performance as doting mothers discuss their children. They are still talking about their horses when it is time to change for dinner. Unlike other members of the Royal Family, Princess Anne does not take her dresser on such informal visits (she knows the pressure a maid and a detective put on the bedrooms, already stretched with a large house-party), but the old housekeeper, who has been in service since long before the War, has unpacked for her.

Dinner that night is just the house-party and a few volunteers running the horse trials. Guests rise as Princess Anne and her husband enter the room. She is offered a drink from the tray, but her hostess knows that she only drinks Coca-Cola. It is a fun evening. It is totally informal—after dinner, guests can even leave before Princess Anne has retired to bed. Some slip away when she throws on her old tweed coat, hitches up her long skirt and trips out to the stables for a last look at the horses.

That week-end, as indeed throughout her life, Princess Anne has little time for herself. She never stops meeting people; she is always on view. Principally, she is a guest in a house-party who is competing in top-level three-day eventing, but however private the occasion, she is still a member of the Royal Family, and is, of course, treated as such. She has the protection of the local police force, (when she is present, it is the county, not the organisers of the horse trials, who pay for them).

Early on Saturday morning, Princess Anne trots her young horse out of the stableyard, immaculate in her black, swallow-tail coat and silk hat and heads towards the dressage arena. Those spectators who have come principally to see her are not fooled by the early start and already flank the arena, just as they will stand by the jumps on the cross-country course, cameras at the ready, hoping for a Royal snap at best, a Royal fall at worst. A brave press photographer chances a quick photograph on the way up; he is rewarded by an ice-cold glance. She is always newsworthy, and, although press photographers are banned from the stableyard, they know they can take their candid photographs at any time through the pierced stonework of the eighteenth-century arch.

Just after lunch, a stand-up buffet in the dining-room, Princess Anne is off again in the intermediate cross-country course—twenty-three fences over three and half miles. It is a good, galloping course, with well-built fences around the park and part of the gardens. Mark Phillips drives his Range Rover to the best vantage points to watch her all the way round. The muffled sound of the commentator charts her progress round the park, and gives her time as she crosses the finishing line. Not a bad time, but nothing special: it is many years since she has had a top-class horse. The groom, puffed out like a Michelin man in a Range Rover anorak, takes her horse as she goes to weigh-in.

For the rest of the day, her time should be her own, but it never is. There is always somebody who would like to meet her, or whom it would be politic to meet. There are the Chief Inspector and the more senior of his colleagues who need a civil word. Then there are the sponsors, and their wives, to be presented to her. She knows first-hand their value to a horse trials and how to steer the conversation, for she and Mark Phillips have their own event at their Gloucestershire home, Gatcombe Park, sponsored by Croft Sherry. She knows too, the value of volunteer labour—fence judges, time-keepers, men in charge of the car-park, the local schoolchildren who pick up the fences in the show jumping arena, the local Yeomanry who man the communications, all of whom need a friendly word. She may even run into some of her own family, her cousins, the Duke and Duchess of Gloucester who live close by, as they drive round the course in their Mini Moke. After watching a good round by Mark Phillips, she retires to her room to put in some work on a speech she has to deliver the next day.

She comes down for tea and a quick scan of the results board. There are more presentations, more photographs, until she can escape to the sanctuary of the drawing room. That night, there is a large dinner-party. They sit down nearly thirty—the grander neighbours, a sprinkling of foreign competitors, the friends who are competing. Those senior members of the country society deem it their right to be placed next to her at dinner. They are charmed by her, she not giving away that she would much sooner be talking about eventing to her contemporaries than listening to how much better life was before the War. It comes easily to her from a childhood spent in the company of her parents' generation.

The next morning, Sunday, the organisers have arranged for Princess Anne to go first in the show-jumping ring as she is lunching in the mess of one of her regiments in Wiltshire. The jumping only takes a few minutes, she collects ten penalty points for two fences down. It is still only nine o'clock. The rush is on to be off so as to arrive in time for her engagement one hundred and twenty miles away. Changed into a smart suit, her hair put up by herself, she says goodbye to her hostess for another year. She signs the visitors' book just "Anne"—unlike other members of the Royal Family, she does not take a separate page for her signature, merely signing under the last guest.

With her detective in the passenger seat, she leaves in her car, a Reliant Scimitar, shadowed by a dark-brown Rover with tell-tale aerials on the roof. A photographer takes a last photograph of her: he captures her set jaw and determined look as she tries to ignore him. As she speeds off, the photographer telephones in his story of how the Princess left early in a foul mood and without saying goodbye to her husband (he was riding the cross-country course at the time). The editor immediately spikes the story—there is no mileage today in perpetuating the old chestnut of a breakdown of their marriage.

The horse trials over, the Team Range Rover box is loaded up for the drive back to Gatcombe Park. Mark Phillips leaves soon after with a winner's rosette and a second. For Princess Anne, it is a shorter drive back to Gatcombe. She arrives in time for tea with her children, Peter, on holiday from his prep school, and Zara. She has put a lot into that week-end, one that was supposed to be informal and relaxed. But then she always does.

1

In the Beginning

BY the evening of 20 August 1950, there can have been few in Britain who did not know of the birth of the Infant Princess. The all-night vigil of the crowd, still damp from the showers that morning, was rewarded by hearing the news direct from the Queen [the present Queen Elizabeth the Queen Mother] when she, in a state of high excitement, mouthed "It's a girl" as her car swept through the tall, black gates of Clarence House. Soon after, the official bulletin, signed by those who attended the birth, was posted on the railings:

Her Royal Highness the Princess Elizabeth, Duchess of Edinburgh, was safely delivered of a Princess at 11.50 a.m. today. Her Royal Highness and daughter are doing well.
(*signed*) William Gilliat, John H. Peel, Vernon F. Hall, John Weir

Later, so many swarmed outside Clarence House to read the bulletin that extra police had to be drafted in to make way for the steady stream of messengers who came to deliver the hundreds of congratulatory telegrams and flowers. Others read of the birth when the same bulletin was placed outside the Mansion House, in the City of London; another was fastened to the railings of the Home Office, in Whitehall.

If those in London on that day had not read the news, they certainly heard the guns. The King's Troop, Royal Horse Artillery, fired their salute of forty-one guns in Hyde Park, (twenty-one for the Royal salute and a further twenty as Hyde Park is designated a Royal saluting station). Soon after, another salute was fired from the Tower of London by the First Regiment, the Honourable Artillery Company. The battery commander was surely hoarse after barking the orders to fire sixty-two guns—two Royal salutes of twenty-one guns and another twenty after the cannonades traditionally fired from each of the towers within the Tower of London. The Royal Navy was not to be outdone. Twenty-one guns boomed out across the Plymouth Sound from the aircraft-carrier HMS *Illustrious*, followed by another from the veteran battleship HMS *Howe*. The Royal Citadel on the Hoe followed that with another salvo. Throughout London and the country, bell-ringers were called to their churches to ring their carillons in celebration of the news.

With a true sense of an occasion, play was even interrupted at the Oval during the Test Match between England and the West Indians for the commentator to announce, "Ladies and Gentlemen—we have a new baby Princess". A great cheer went up from both field and spectators before play was resumed.

The Home Secretary, Chuter Ede, was officially notified by telephone of the birth by a member of the Princess's Household. Formerly, he would have been at Clarence House, but the seventeenth-century tradition of having a Minister of the Crown present at the birth (at least in the house), of one in line to the throne was discontinued when Prince Charles was born. With Parliament in summer recession, Mr. Ede was also robbed of his prerogative to break the news to the House of Commons. Instead, he had to be content with officially informing the Lord Mayor of London, who knew already, having instructed the bulletin to be posted outside Mansion House.

Messengers were dispatched from Clarence House with letters to each Ambassador at the Court of St. James, for them to pass on the news to their respective countries. Likewise, the private post office in Buckingham Palace was busy sending telegrams to every Governor-General throughout the dominions and colonies.

Such a national display of enthusiasm for a Royal event was, and still is, very much a part of British life. The country had drawn great strength from the King and Queen during the Second World War, massing in front of

3

Buckingham Palace in time of crisis, as well as in victory. The wedding of Princess Elizabeth to Lieutenant Philip Mountbatten was a bright occasion in a still drab post-War Britain, and the birth of Prince Charles, almost two years later, was another great cause for celebration. So the birth of the infant princess, still officially unnamed although third in line to the throne, was marked with equal fervour, heralded in the press as the spirit of the new era and of the second half of the century.

However important the parents, or public the interest, a birth is primarily a family affair. With the birth of Prince Charles, the succession was secure so the arrival of the second child was that much more relaxed. It had been coyly surmised that Princess Elizabeth was pregnant again in the spring of 1950 when she returned to Clarence House from Malta, where she had been enjoying the life of the wife of a serving Royal Navy officer rather than that of the daughter of the King. Prince Philip followed her home in July. On the morning of 15 August, he waited patiently downstairs—not for him the role of the modern father and being present at the actual birth. Later, he toasted the health of his new-born daughter in champagne with members of the Household. For him, it was a double celebration as that morning he had been gazetted Lieutenant-Commander and given his own command, HMS *Magpie*, a frigate in the Mediterranean Fleet. He can only have forgotten the excitement of that morning when, years later, he surmised that "People want their first child very much when they marry, they want their second child almost as much. If a third comes along, they accept it as natural."

The Duke was certainly proud of his daughter, declaring her the "sweetest girl" when he telephoned his grandmother, the Dowager Marchioness of Milford Haven, at Kensington Palace. She then passed the news to his mother, Princess Andrew, who was staying with her. He telephoned Balmoral and the message was carried breathlessly to the King, who was shooting (grouse) on a distant moor. That night he travelled to Balmoral to deliver the good news in person. Another call went to Drumlanrig Castle, Dumfriesshire, where Princess Margaret was staying with the Duke and Duchess of Buccleuch. Similar calls were made to other near relations, including the many German cousins on the Continent.

What should have been news for a day or two, the press prolonged for months, filling their scant pages with speculative articles on life at Clarence House. Readers were regaled with facts, mostly trivial—how, despite Princess Elizabeth's annual income of £50,000, "there will be few new clothes for the princess" (as if to console every other family in the country struggling on clothing coupons), or "as this is their second

5

child, the couple will now be entitled to the five shillings [25p] family allowance". They reported the presents that flooded into Clarence House, the knitted baby clothes by the sackful, and the toys and dolls. Everything was news. Cassandra, the legendary columnist of the *Daily Mirror*, wrote prophetically that if the Princess could read, "I am sure that she would let out a yell of laughter in derision or pure rage at the words of excruciating goo that have been written about her in the past forty-eight hours."

Another wave of "princess mania" was sparked off when her names were announced: Anne Elizabeth Alice Louise, or to give her her full title, Her Royal Highness Princess Anne Elizabeth Alice Louise of Edinburgh. Like every other parent, they chose the names, with or without a family connection, that they liked, yet much has been written about the choice of Charles and Anne as being a romantic revival of the Stuart names. The names, chosen simply for personal and private reasons, were approved of by the King who, surprisingly, found them "unusual". Elizabeth, being her mother and grandmother's name, was an obvious choice, as was Alice, after her paternal grandmother. It is more likely that Louise was chosen as a tribute to the Royal Family's favourite uncle and mentor, the late Lord Louis Mountbatten than to Princess Elizabeth's great-aunt, Princess

Louise, daughter of Edward VII and penultimate Princess Royal.

These names were given to her by her sponsors (Royal godparents), her two grandmothers, her aunt, Princess Margarita of Hohenlohe Langenburg, Lord Louis Mountbatten and the Reverend the Hon. Andrew Elphinstone, her mother's first cousin at her christening, a month after her birth. It was very much a family affair in the best Royal traditions—the Music Room of Buckingham Palace, the Jordan water in the Lilly Font, the Honiton lace robes that have been used since Edward VII was christened and still used today. The only departure from the norm came when the Archbishop of York, Dr. Garbett, deputised for the Archbishop of Canterbury, Dr. Fisher, who was in Australia. Cecil Beaton took the photographs, declaring that she was a "small baby with quite a definite nose for one so young, large, sleepy, grey-green eyes and a particularly pretty mouth." One nice touch to the christening was that the Duke of Edinburgh brought his Maltese steward, Vincent, to watch the baptism and later introduced him to his uncle.

For the next sixteen months, life at Clarence House was remarkably well-ordered, despite a busy working mother and a father on active service abroad in the Royal Navy. After Prince Charles was born, Princess Elizabeth was given a year free from official engagements to devote to family life, but, as the King was far from well, she could not be spared. However, once she had finished nursing Princess Anne she was able to rejoin her husband in Malta that first Christmas. That short absence of her mother can have meant nothing to the four-month-old baby, but the frequent tours made by her parents throughout her childhood, often for months at a time, was something that she had to endure. But then, that was just a part of her life as a member of the Royal family.

During those early trips abroad, Princess Anne and her brother were left in the charge of her grandparents and the nursery staff. No extra staff had been engaged for Princess Anne, a nanny and nursery maid being thought quite adequate for a two-year-old boy and a new baby. Miss Helen Lightbody (as nanny she was accorded the courtesy title of "Mrs.") had been in Royal service for some time, having come from Barnwell, where she had been outgrown by the Duke and Duchess of Gloucester's two boys, William and Richard. It did not take long for the nursery maid, Mabel Anderson, the daughter of a Liverpool policeman, to become part of the Royal nursery team, a place she held for many years and from which she has only comparatively recently retired.

The nurseries at Clarence House were on the top floor, recently redecorated in pale blue and furnished in a style identical to Princess Elizabeth's nursery at her parents' first London home, 145 Piccadilly. Nanny Lightbody set up a routine in her nursery that was pre-War in style and inflexibility. An early start at seven o'clock was followed by breakfast at eight, before being taken downstairs at nine o'clock to their parents' bedrooms for half an hour. The rest of the day was interspersed with rests, invariably in a pram outside, and healthy walks, whatever the weather. Although Prince Philip was disappointed to be recalled from the command of his ship to help with the increased workload caused by the King's illness, he at least was at home with his wife and children. Engagements and nanny permitting, both he and Princess Elizabeth saw as much of their children as possible, "always popping in and out of the nursery". Anne would have been far too young to remember the week-ends spent at Windlesham Moor, the house her parents rented in Berkshire, or those early holidays within the "Royal migration"—Sandringham for Christmas, Windsor for Easter, and Birkhall, the Queen Mother's present home near Balmoral, for late summer and early autumn.

When Anne was just over a year old, her parents were abroad again for an official visit to Canada and the United States and once again, she was in the nominal charge of her grandparents. Christmas that year, 1951, was spent as usual at Sandringham, somewhat blighted with

Princess Elizabeth and the Duke of Edinburgh's preparations for their forthcoming Commonwealth Tour in February. When they said their good-byes to the sixteen-month-old Anne at Sandringham, she can have had little idea that her parents were going away for so long. She would not have registered the pictures in the newspapers, nor the television news of their departure from Heathrow Airport, but she heard it first-hand from her grandparents the next day. Three days later, the King came in from the annual hare shoot, had his tea and a short rest. For the first time ever, he went up to the nursery where Charles and Anne were having their supper. He stayed with them, then knelt with them as they said their prayers before tucking them up and saying goodnight. In the early hours of the morning, 6 February, he died quietly in his sleep. At that moment, Princess Elizabeth became Queen Elizabeth II.

Being the daughter of the Queen, as opposed to the daughter of the heir presumptive, initially made little difference to Anne. The only real changes were of no importance to her then (or now)—she was second in line to the throne and fourth woman in the realm, she was also accorded the title of *The* Princess Anne, as daughter of the sovereign. Apart from that, the daily routine was very much the same. For the first few months, she still lived at Clarence House, her mother who tucked her up in bed was still exactly the same woman. They went, as usual, to Windsor for Easter. Even at that age, Anne had become used to moving every few months to a different house, so when Clarence House, a large but comfortable home, was exchanged for the smaller, more austere apartments at Buckingham Palace, it cannot have meant anything to her. The Queen, remembering her own move there in 1936, had the second-floor nurseries redecorated to look as much as possible like those at Clarence House and had all the nursery furniture brought over.

The consensus of Royal biographers' views of that period is of a young Queen, burdened by affairs of state and "robbed" of the enjoyment of her very young children, for, had it not been for the early death of her father, she could have reasonably expected her life as Heir Presumptive to have continued for at least another fifteen years. Examples are given of how Charles and Anne tried to persuade their mother to come and play, and the Queen, like a child who has not completed her difficult homework, replies (sadly), "If only I could." It is of course true that, at the age of twenty-five, she was prematurely launched into her role as sovereign. Although nothing, not even family, would ever sway her from her duty as Queen first, she was still the mother of her two young children. The same was true of her father. Far from being deprived of attention from her mother and father

11

as Queen and consort, Anne probably saw more of her parents than most of her contemporaries from aristocratic and landed backgrounds saw of theirs. The Queen made a point of being at home, whenever possible, when her children were going to bed—she even asked her Prime Minister, Winston Churchill, to delay his weekly audience by one hour so as not to miss bath-time. After the King died, the Court was in mourning for six months which was spent quietly at home. The Queen knew, and knows, exactly what she will be doing, almost to the hour, for six months in advance, so it was not hard for her to work out when she could be with her offspring. Week-ends were spent, as a family, at Windsor. There were the long holidays too, six weeks at Sandringham, four weeks at Windsor and ten weeks at Balmoral, virtually free from engagements and public duties when the family were together. The Queen still had her "boxes" and attended to matters of State, but, being an early riser, she dealt with those early in the morning, leaving the rest of the day free. The only hint of a busy, public life at home, or in any of the Royal residences, was that the Queen's study was barred to both children—but then so was the "business room" of any sizeable country house. By the time her sons Andrew and Edward were old enough to crawl, even that rule had been waived. The one forced separation was during the Coronation Tour of the Commonwealth in 1953 which lasted nearly six months. Although of course they missed their parents, Charles and Anne were surrounded by family— the Queen Mother and Princess Margaret at Clarence House and their paternal grandmother, Princess Andrew at Buckingham Palace. They spoke almost daily to their parents by telephone, and had the excitement of letters and postcards from all parts of the world. As a special treat, they were allowed to meet them at Malta on their way home.

Her position as a Royal Princess did not affect Anne either. The Queen had instructed the Household and staff at all the Royal residences to call her by her Christian name only, (she remained "Anne" to them until a discreet note went round the staff on her eighteenth birthday stating that the Queen wished for her to be addressed as Ma'am and referred to as "Princess Anne"). The same applied to acts of obeisance. No one curtseyed or bowed to her as a Princess, just as she did not curtsey to her mother as Queen. Again, the Queen remembered when her father returned as King after the public proclamation and she and Princess Margaret dropped low curtseys to him, how much he disliked it in his daughters. The only exception for Anne was in the presence of Queen Mary, who never approved of such dispensations. Anne, likewise, did not approve of such decorum. When taken to visit her great-grandmother, whom she called

Gan-Gan, she steadfastly refused to curtsey, and, according to Anthony Holden "shyly hung her head, scuffed the carpet with her shoes and looked vague". It was seen as a very early sign of an independent nature.

Where Anne was treated as any other little girl within the Palace, she was still the daughter of the Queen. Her parents were just the latest in a long line of those members of the Royal Family who strove to bring up their children as individuals and to prepare them for a rapidly changing world, as far as possible unaffected by their Royal trappings. Because of who they are and what they stand for, as well as living in such a rarefied atmosphere, the Royal Family are naturally different to the rest of their subjects; it is impossible for them not to be. As Anne obviously did not know of any other life than that of a member of the Royal Family, she did not consider herself any different to any other child. Like every child, Royal or commoner, she took her position for granted. What that position was slowly dawned on her when, outside the Palace grounds, people showed a great interest in her and her family. Princess Anne was asked on the radio programme *Tuesday Call* if she knew as a child that she was a princess or if she ever played at being one. She admitted that she never played at being a princess. "I am not quite sure why, I don't know *when* you know as a child, but you appreciate what you are, or if you have a title what that means; but I'm afraid 'no' —I don't think a princess is anything I ever played at really. I have probably been playing it ever since!"

Her early companions who came to Buckingham Palace every week for dancing classes under Mme. Vacani, were the children of her parents' friends and the Household, all of whom came from privileged backgrounds. Although they did not live in palaces with a nursery footman, they all had nannies: Charles, aged five, once asked a little boy standing with his mother if she was his nanny. What she *did* have in common with every other family was that she was thrown together with her brother, sometimes with the inevitable sibling rivalry. With two children so close in age, it is only natural to think that they should be friends and wish to play together. But there is, however, no biological law that states that children should prefer their brothers or sisters to an outsider. For both Anne and Charles, there were no accessible outsiders, at least of their own age. Apart from those little friends specially imported to the Palace, Anne had to rely solely on the company of her brother, and members of her family, the Household and the staff for her friends.

Although her parents went out of their way not to show favouritism between any of their children, it must have been extremely difficult for Anne as a second child. In 1980 Princess

Anne admitted in a revealing interview with Kenneth Harris in the *Observer* that she "always accepted the role of being second in everything from quite an early age. You adopt that position as part of that experience. You start off in life very much a tail-end Charlie, at the back of the line." Wherever she started, she was soon to come to the fore. She had all the competitiveness of a second child, yet, at that stage of their lives, the competition was barely up to her standard. She could not have been more different to her brother in character and temperament which, throughout their childhoods, made for an affectionate, but often combustible, relationship. Again, much has been written on how Anne has taken after her father, while her brother is more like their mother. No child is an exact clone of either parent, although certain of Prince Philip's more forceful characteristics were, and are, very marked in Anne, just as the Queen's reserved nature has come out in Charles. As children, they were complete opposites—Charles, meek and defensive, his sister, strong-willed and extrovert; where he was bashful and withdrawn, she was petulant and haughty. Mabel Anderson found that "he was never as boisterous or noisy as Princess Anne. She had a much stronger, more extrovert personality. She didn't exactly push him aside, but she was certainly a more forceful child."

Comparisons between them were all too

evident. Those Mall-watchers noted that it was Anne who waved to the crowds with a confidence that belied her years while her older brother pressed himself into the back seat of the car out of sight. She has been cited as being thoughtless compared to her brother; for example, it was the well-mannered Charles who took her by the hand to thank the engine-driver who drove them to Sandringham. Such courtesies only happen in Royal circles and are all part of the preparation for later life. Charles, who had learned that particular lesson, was only passing it on to his sister. Another favourite story is of how she, like her mother, delighted in the well-practised trick of walking past the sentries so that they would present arms to her. What girl of any spirit would not walk past long-suffering sentries if her presence produced such startling results? By contrast, Charles always made a wide detour of the sentry-boxes.

It cannot have helped either that Anne was physically more robust than her brother. When Prince Philip gave them each a pair of boxing gloves, they had to be taken away from her before she inflicted serious damage on her brother. When William, a strawberry-roan pony, was delivered to the Royal Mews, it was Anne who took him over, even though it was supposed to be a shared present. She appeared to be fearless. Conflict, particularly Royal conflict in the nursery, makes for a better story than a scene of domestic harmony. There are quarrels in every family, Princess Anne even admitting in retrospect that she and her brother "fought like cats and dogs". Such discord can not have been as bad as she remembers it, as they spent all their time together, at least when Charles was not in the schoolroom.

Anne always was, and still is, very active. Despite her appearance, a mass of fair curls and blue eyes, she was a tom-boy. She dressed in sensible clothes—not for her pretty dresses, but practical jeans and sweaters. She disliked dolls, although it was thought better if she was photographed with them. Once, when asked the name of a doll in her pram, she replied, "No name!" Her one concession to the supposed little girl addiction to dolls was her delight in playing in Y Bwthyn Bach, a miniature Welsh cottage in the grounds of Royal Lodge, the Queen Mother's home within Windsor Great Park. It was a perfect quarter-sized thatched cottage given to her mother by a Welsh consortium. Instead, "having an elder brother . . . I was rather more interested in playing the sort of games that he was playing, rather than anything else." She could also amuse herself. She was good with her hands and adept at an early age at one of the Royal Family's favourite pastimes—jigsaw puzzles. Even now, there is always a large and difficult jigsaw on a table wherever the Royal Family is in residence.

In her biography of her cousin, Prince Philip, Queen Alexandria of Yugoslavia wrote that she "was sure that he [Prince Philip] was aware that he did not see enough of his father. He always wanted to 'make this up' to his children." He spent hours instructing them, but again, it was Anne who was the quicker pupil. He taught them both to swim in the pools at Buckingham Palace and Windsor, but it was Anne who took to sailing with him, on his yachts *Bloodhound*, *Cowslip* and *Bluebottle* and on the little catamaran on Loch Muick.

But Anne did not have it all her own way. After the initial excitement of having a baby sister had worn off, Charles soon realised that he no longer had the undivided attention of his parents and his nannies. However, he still had all the advantages of being the elder child (by the same token, Princess Anne later said she was "delighted that I did not have a sister"). Not that she would have shown it then, but Charles has always been the Queen Mother's favourite grandchild. To the fury of his sister, it was Charles who went to the Coronation at Westminster Abbey while she was left behind to watch on television. Princess Anne dimly remembers the day, not the tantrum, and being taken out on the balcony of Buckingham Palace and told to wave. Even at that age, that rich Hanoverian temper was there. Princess Alice, Duchess of Gloucester, recalled the five-year-old

Anne plunging a dirk through the eiderdown, sheets and blankets into the mattress of a guest's [empty] bed at Balmoral, saying: "I've always wanted to do this!"

Although the Duke of Edinburgh is consort to the Queen, he has always been, naturally, the head of his family. It was he who made certain that none of his children was spoilt, something that Nanny Lightbody was pleased to concur with. Punctuality for all meals was imperative—breakfast at eight o'clock, lunch at noon, tea at four o'clock with milk and biscuits at six. When Anne was having her portrait painted, the artist was shocked to see the three-year-old denied a sweet biscuit at their mid-morning break—only plain biscuits were allowed in the morning. When old enough, they all made their beds.

What may appear a strict upbringing by today's standards, was par for the course for any child of a privileged family of the fifties. But the Royal Family, by dint of being Royal, are a very close-knit and protective family. The Queen's own childhood was also exceptionally happy, but not without her father's occasional "gnashes" (George VI's famous rages), while Prince Philip's childhood was somewhat less secure after his exiled father separated from his mother. So her parents, influenced by their own childhoods, created a secure and warm atmosphere for Anne and her brothers to grow up in. Prince Charles has always thought of his family "as very special people. I've never wanted not to have a home life—to get away from home. I love my home life. We happen to be a very close-knit family. I'm happier at home with my family than anywhere else." Unlike her brother, Princess Anne was not besotted with her family, at least, not initially. She admitted again to Kenneth Harris, that "as a child and up to my teens, I don't think that I went along with the family bit, not until later than anyone else. I know its value now, but I don't think I did up to my middle teens." The benefits of that early home life are something that, with a family of her own, she has only now come fully to appreciate: "The greatest advantage of my entire life is the family I grew up in. I'm eternally thankful for being able to grow up in the sort of atmosphere that was given to me—and to have it to continue now that I am grown up . . ."

Besides that exceptionally happy home, the advantages of Anne's Royal upbringing must surely have outweighed the many disadvantages. Each of the four Royal residences is grand in its own way, each is filled with some of the finest collections of pictures and furniture ever produced. They are all fully staffed. Buckingham Palace is set in a beautiful garden of thirty-nine acres in the middle of London; the country residences, Windsor, Sandringham and Balmoral, are all surrounded by large agricultural estates. But what child appreciates their surroundings

21

until later in life? Despite her parents' expert knowledge and enthusiasm, as a child, Anne merely took it all for granted, just as she took her modes of travelling for granted. Two chauffeurs, a detective and a nanny accompanied her in a car; she and Charles had their own carriage in the Royal Train (at least until 1955 when it was discontinued, and four coaches were merely tacked on to the rear of an ordinary train). She went in aircraft of the Queen's Flight on longer journeys. Some of her birthdays (mid-August), were spent cruising the Western Isles of Scotland aboard the Royal yacht *Britannia*. But, to Anne and her parents' credit, "privilege" read "opportunity" and they made the most of that.

Against those advantages, there was the constant demand from the public, fostered by the press, to see her. They demanded photographs and newsreels, stories and appearances. The Queen, remembering her own childhood, did not give in to these demands too readily (even less with her two youngest sons). With no precedent to follow, the young Duchess of York (the present Queen Mother) often indulged the public's demand to see her elder daughter, so much so that she once admitted that "it almost frightens me that the people should love her so much. I suppose it is a good thing . . ." Mindful of her own upbringing, Princess Anne has been even more protective towards her own children than her mother was with her.

The greatest disadvantage of all is surely that same problem faced by generations of Royal parents: how to bring up their children as "normal" as possible within the Royal framework. It was nothing new—the Duke of Windsor summed it up in his autobiography when he wrote, "The pleased incredulity with which the public reacts to the elementary demonstrations on the part of Royalty that they are, after all, like other people is matched only by the public's firm refusal to accept them as such."

Prince Philip instantly recognised the problem and accepted it as an unalterable fact. His children were not the same as ordinary children, as he explained to Basil Boothroyd: "People talk about a normal upbringing. What is a normal upbringing? What you really mean is: was I insisting that they should go through all the disadvantages in being brought up in the way other people are brought up? Precisely that—disadvantages. There's always this idea about treating them exactly like other children. In fact it means that they are treated much worse, because they're known by name and association . . . it is all very well to say they're treated the same as everybody else, but it's impossible."

So, instead of fighting against that "accident of birth" the Queen and Prince Philip recognised the situation and acted upon it. The two areas where their children might find companionship

23

outside the family and Household were at school and within the Royal Family's old stand-by, the Girl Guide movement. Historically, Royal children were taught by tutors and governesses, brothers and sisters being herded into the schoolroom together, regardless of age or ability. For Anne, the system had already been revived with Miss Catherine Peebles who had been engaged as Charles's governess when he was not quite five years old. "Mispy" was a typical Royal choice. A Scotswoman by birth, she was used to Royal service having come from teaching the Duchess of Kent's two youngest children, Princess Alexandra and Prince Michael. She had good common sense as opposed to academic qualifications, which were, in fact, nil. Anne was barred from the schoolroom for the first two years, while her brother struggled with his lessons alone. She joined him, or as she says, "just tagged along", up to the time he left to go to his London day-prep school. His place was then taken by two girls, Susan (known as Sukie) Babington-Smith and Caroline Hamilton.

These two girls were an excellent choice of companions for Anne. They were both bright and jolly, and, more important, they were her exact contemporaries. They were connected to the Royal network, but not too closely so as to cause any embarrassment should the arrangement not work out (Sukie is the grand-daughter of Admiral the Hon. Sir Hubert Meads-

24

Featherstonhaugh, equerry to George V, while Caroline is the grand-daughter of the then Dean of Windsor). The arrangement did work and lasted for seven years, when they went to their separate schools.

The system was especially beneficial for Anne. Being so self-assured, she could easily have coped at any London day-school, but her parents thought, quite correctly in retrospect, that this was the better method. It was a splendid education, on all counts. With only three pupils, Anne had the benefit of virtual individual tuition in the schoolroom at Buckingham Palace, or Balmoral for the first four weeks of the autumn term. For anything outside Mispy's capabilities, like French or music, extra tutors were brought in. Lessons were held in the school-room during the morning, leaving the afternoons free for expeditions. Again, in that Anne was especially fortunate, and she made the most of her opportunities. As the daughter of the Queen, she naturally received Royal treatment. Not for her and her little companions the queuing to see the Tower of London. Instead, she was received by the Governor and shown round by the chief Yeoman Warder. Every year, when they went to Wimbledon, it was the front row of the Royal Box and tea in the ante-room behind, often with a centre-court "idol". When they went skating at Richmond Ice Rink, they had the place to themselves and the best instructress—Betty

Callaway, the trainer of the world ice skating champions, Torvill and Dean. They had the best seats at the Planetarium, the director of the London Zoo took them round himself, and so on through all the things that children are taken to in London. It can only have been strange for a small girl to visit Mme. Tussaud's wax museum and see not only her parents and brother, but some of her forebears for nearly a thousand years.

Public interest in the Royal children was insatiable. During Charles' first term at Cheam, there were sixty-eight stories in the newspapers in eighty-eight days. Anne, less accessible in Buckingham Palace, was more fortunate. However, on her ninth birthday, an "insider's view" appeared in the *Daily Telegraph*:

She continues to do lessons every morning during term time at Buckingham Palace with her governess, Miss Peebles, and her two friends . . . Lessons cover the usual subjects for a child of her age. The Princess particularly enjoys history lessons and last term started studying the reign of Elizabeth I. She also enjoys geography and studying maps. During the Canadian tour by the Queen and Prince Philip, she followed her parents' progress on a map of Canada, flagging the map as they reached each new place. She now has regular French lessons. The Princess continues

26

to have weekly sessions of piano lessons, and dancing classes are held at the Palace for a small class to learn ballroom and ballet dancing.

The Princess has also a weekly gym lesson and this term had a few tennis lessons on the Buckingham Palace tennis courts. She is a keen swimmer and bathes as often as possible in the Palace swimming-bath. She was taught to swim by Prince Philip but has not yet learned to dive.

The Princess has a pony at Balmoral so that she can join in the riding there. At Windsor during the past year she has been riding regularly at weekends, sometimes taking small jumps. She is also a keen cyclist and her bicycle is at Balmoral too.

One of the great excitements of the past year was the revival of the Buckingham Palace Brownie pack. After a few meetings, she was duly enrolled as a "Pixie" by her great-aunt, the Princess Royal (President of the Girl Guides' Association).

Princess Anne, like most children, enjoys watching television, reading adventure stories and having someone read to her.

The "1st B/ham Palace Pack" was formed from twelve girls from the Holy Trinity Pack, Anne and her two companions and a few of the children of various members of the Household and staff. The "outsiders" included the daughters of a taxi driver and a hotel maintenance engineer. Whatever their origins, none was intimidated by the grandness of the Palace (they met in the summer house in the grounds or, if wet, in the room used for the cinema) or by Anne. That said, it is to her credit that they voted her Patrol Leader, a position she gained through merit, as opposed to position, both as a Brownie and later, as a Girl Guide.

For Anne, the birth of Prince Andrew in 1960 was more significant than just the excitement of the arrival of a baby brother. She moved down a place from being second in line of succession, (with Prince Edward and now the Prince of Wales's two sons, William and Harry, she is today, sixth in line). Consciously or subconsciously, Princess Margaret certainly suffered from being female and second in line of succession to her elder sister. For the first ten years of her life, lines of succession meant little to Anne, but at least she was spared any problem in the future. Also, with the birth of Andrew, she was no longer the youngest member of the Royal Family.

At the age of twelve, Anne had outgrown the schoolroom and her restrictive life bounded by the railings of Buckingham Palace. All that she knew of an un-Royal life came second-hand, from her companions, the girls in the Brownie Pack and at the two Girl Guide camps she attended in the summer, and from her brother, who had left Cheam and was battling with the rigours of Gordonstoun in the north of Scotland. As a father, Prince Philip gave his children the opportunity to do things. "He says: 'We think it might be an idea; what do you think?'" Her parents thought that it "might be an idea" if Anne went away to school, like her cousin, Princess Alexandra, and put the suggestion to her. She readily agreed although she later admitted that it would not have made much difference if she had said "no". Anne went to Benenden, a girls' boarding-school in Kent, shortly after her thirteenth birthday. So began the next stage of her life.

2

To School

BENENDEN proved an admirable choice
of school for Anne. Academically, it rated
among the top five girls' schools in the
country—it even had a special course for girls
who wanted to take up medicine as a career
which, for one day, sent the press into a frenzy
of excitement as they suggested that Anne was
to become a nurse. Benenden's position was of
even greater importance. Set in the High Weald
of Kent near the small town of Cranbrook, it
was close enough to London for easy visiting by
the Queen and Prince Philip, but far enough
away, and difficult to drive to, for most of the
press. Charles had suffered from a virtual siege
of reporters and photographers when he first
went to Cheam, so it was only the most ardent
who were to bother Anne there. It was also close
to Horsted Place, near Uckfield, the home of the
Queen and Prince Philip's friend and courtier,
Lord Rupert Nevill and his family. Their house
was a useful base for Anne at weekends if she
needed it, and her parents when they came to
take her out. The Queen Mother was also
pleased with the choice as the school was close

to Fairlawne, the home of her friend and trainer, Major Peter Cazalet. She was not above dropping in by helicopter on her way to or from an engagement in the area.

The headmistress, Miss Elizabeth Clarke, had been asked to an informal lunch at Windsor Castle to meet her prospective pupil and her parents. A few days later, the Queen telephoned her and asked if she would take Anne. Her answer was not automatic. Most girls have to pass Common Entrance to go to a public school, but in Anne's case, this was waived as her early education did not include examinations. Instead, Miss Clarke spoke to Miss Peebles and her other tutors who satisfied her of Anne's academic ability. Had she not been at the same standard as the other girls, "it would have been unfair to the school and we would not have been doing her any favours".

That first evening of the Michaelmas term, 20 September 1963, the whole school of three hundred girls and forty staff turned out to greet the Queen and the new pupil, a one-off concession to her rank. No child who has been away to school can ever forget that dreadful, sinking feeling on first day of term at a new school. For Anne, with her sheltered background, it can only have been ten times worse. The Royal car, usually arriving on time to the exact second, was late. It had been delayed a few minutes on the way while Anne was sick,

31

through nerves. Dressed in her school uniform, she was welcomed by the headmistress, and introduced to her housemistress, Miss Cynthia Gee, the head girl and her "house mother", Elizabeth Somershield, a second-term girl detailed to show her the "ropes". The Queen's comment after her half-hour stay was that: "The girls look so alike in their uniform that I don't know whether I shall be able to pick out Princess Anne when I come next." That, of course, was precisely the idea. She should become an integral part of her new surroundings.

The initial shock of entering a girls' boarding school must have been greater than even Anne could have imagined. She shared the Magnolia Room in the Bachelor's Wing with three other girls. The accommodation was typically Spartan, with picture-less green and white walls, and a plain varnished wood floor. Beside her black iron bedstead, was a wooden chair and a dressing table. For Anne, living in an environment which is virtually silent, where servants are rarely seen and certainly not heard, she found the constant bustle and noise of a girls' school "staggering".

Having no idea of what to expect from the other girls, it came as a pleasant surprise to Anne that it was easy to integrate herself into the school. Charles, with his position and temperament, had always found it difficult to make friends at school—boys would hang back for fear of being thought a toady—but Anne had no such problem. With the system of house mothers, girls naturally gravitated initially towards their circle of friends. Anne was no exception, finding hers "a caustic lot who knew exactly what they thought about other people and saved one a lot of embarrassment".

The school helped too, although Miss Gee admitted to having a Royal charge "a bit of a shock, but, we had had a princess at Benenden before—a Danish one [Benedikte]—and after she [Anne] had arrived, it was all perfectly normal". In fact, two other princesses came at the same time as Anne, two of Haile Selassie's grand-daughters, Princesses Mariasina and Sihin, and the sister of the King of Jordan, Princess Masma. Her fellow pupils were instructed to call her "Anne", (the mistresses called her Princess Anne). Every few days, the *placement* in the dining room changed, so, in a few weeks, every girl in the house had sat beside her. One girl in her house, Susan Forgan, recalled that "when she came to Benenden, at first no one dared to talk to her . . . but after a short while we all treated her normally. I never felt that I was talking to the daughter of the Queen . . . she had a very good sense of humour." And Princess Anne said of her first days, "Fortunately, children aren't so stupid. They accept people for what they are rather quicker than adults do. They have no preconceived ideas, because how could they have? They accepted people for what they were and they had other things to do, so they weren't bothered." It is very much a Royal trait that friendship is not given lightly, but when it is, it is a friendship that lasts. Anne, too, was selective in her friendships, and once a real friend was made, she remained. One such Benenden friend is Victoria Legge-Bourke, who is one of her ladies-in-waiting and closest friends today.

With her adaptable nature, it did not take long for Anne to settle into the routine of school life. In common with most boarding-schools then, each day at Benenden was so full that it was impossible for her not to be carried along with the rest of the school. Active by nature, she made the most of what was on offer, at least outside the classroom, but only if it amused her. Of her academic record, Miss Gee said of her after she had left, "I don't think she worked especially hard. She was in no way stupid. In fact, I think that you could say that economy of effort was her watchword." That economy of effort produced two "A" level passes in History and Geography, grades D and E

Anne applied herself more on the games field: "She had a very good games sense. She was in the school second XII at lacrosse and she had a very good idea of who to pass to, and I think that if her stick-work had been better I think that she might have got into the first XII." When her team made it to the All England Schools' Tournament, they won all the matches in their section, but to Anne, the greater triumph was not to be recognised throughout the tournament, rather than any particular achievement. The Queen's remark that all the girls looked alike on the first day of term worked for the press and public. Anne even went skiing in Davos with a school party, undetected. The press discovered too late that she had gone rock-climbing. Again, there is a picture of Anne dividing her time between the classroom and her pony, High Jinks, at the Moat House stables. Miss Gee confirmed that she was very keen but that it was not over-encouraged: "She rode once a week but no more." During the 1981 Wimbledon Championships, the BBC commentator Dan Mascall, seeing Princess Anne in the Royal Box, mentioned that "had she taken up tennis rather than horses, she would have been a top-class player today." Princess Anne did not agree. Although she plays a steady game which she enjoys, she admits to being "temperamentally unsuited to tennis, especially in this day and age".

During those five years at Benenden, Anne blended into the life of the school and its pupils. She learned quickly to cope with others, how to give as well as to take. She learned too not to take things for granted, which, in turn, made for a greater appreciation of what she did have. She was sociable, but, at the same time enjoyed her own company, going off for long walks by herself. There were no concessions to her rank, other than the presence of a detective. Occasionally, she was needed for some Royal function and a day's absence was automatically granted. If it was a family affair, then the request was always turned down. There were no favours, so no precedents set for other pupils. During the holidays, she stayed with her friends, just as they stayed with her at Windsor Castle and Balmoral. In the end, there were only a few marked differences between Anne and her fellow pupils. Where they talked openly about their parents and home life, she was silent. Where other girls went home or to some nearby hotel on their exeats with their parents, Anne went to lunch with men like the Archbishop of Canterbury. Another difference was much in keeping with a Royal Family trait—a positive loathing of spending money. Whereas the rest of the school had gone through their allowances, and more, before the end of term, Anne had not used up her £2.

In her last year, Anne was made Captain of her House. It was no sinecure, but something that came easily to her. Miss Clarke thought her capable and "able to exert her authority in a natural manner without being aggressive. If there was any failing at all it was possibly her impatience. She was extremely quick to grasp things herself and couldn't understand anyone else not being able to do so."

Benenden claims that the final product of their education is not easily identified as they do not try to mould their girls. Their overriding aim is that when their pupils leave, that they should care for other people. In that, they had certainly succeeded with Princess Anne. In return, it was certainly an honour that the Queen's daughter should be educated at Benenden. While they could have done without the press and television coverage, the benefits outweighed the disadvantages. Her headmistress hoped that they, in their turn, "contributed something to her training for her future role in public life".

There never has been a school for Royal training—Princess Anne dismisses the idiotic stories, such as where she was made to stand for hours as a child to practise for her future role, with a bemused smile of incredulity. The only Royal training that exists is achieved solely through association with the various members of the Royal Family; the "lessons" are self-taught, learned by trial and error. By the time Anne left Benenden, she had had a certain amount of international exposure, although mostly at family occasions. She appeared on the balcony of Buckingham Palace after such State occasions as the Trooping the Colour. She was *the* catch as a bridesmaid, acting for her aunt, Princess Margaret, her cousins, the Duke of Kent and

Princess Alexandra, also Lady Pamela Mountbatten. She was much in demand, going to Athens as chief bridesmaid for the wedding of King Constantine of Greece to Princess Anne-Marie of Denmark.

There was no hurry for Anne to begin her public life while she was still at school. However, she was given a taste of what was in store by her parents when they included her in a few of their engagements. An early memory is "tagging along" with them as a small child at some function at Cardiff before boarding the Royal Yacht *Britannia* at Milford Haven. Most of these engagements were abroad, some exciting, like the time she accompanied the Duke of Edinburgh to Jamaica when he opened the Commonwealth Games. It was a great experience, as well as an exotic holiday, where she met the competitors, each a champion in their own right, from all over the Commonwealth. At home, she became well used to meeting the most important people in the country, politicians, service chiefs, the captains of industry and so on. The Prime Minister and his wife stayed at Balmoral for a few days each year; cabinet ministers called at the Palace. She met foreign royalty (mostly related) and heads of state on official visits.

However, once she had left school and decided not to go to university, (her grades were too low in any case for any but one of the reddest-brick hue), Anne was set, if not totally prepared, for a life of public service.

3

Coming of Age

HER eighteenth birthday, spent, as usual, aboard the Royal Yacht *Britannia* cruising off the West Coast of Scotland, was particularly significant for Princess Anne. School was behind her, and she was not going to university. The directive had gone round from the Queen to Household and staff that she was now *Princess* Anne and to be called "Ma'am" or "Your Royal Highness". By any eighteen-year-old's standards she was well-off, being granted £15,000 from the Civil List. She had her own suite of rooms, and a sitting-room shared with her brother at Buckingham Palace. She had a driving licence—having driven on the Royal estate roads since the age of nine, she passed her driving test easily. She also had her own new car, a Rover 2000, a birthday present (two months late) from her parents. Most important of all, she was part of what George VI called the "family firm", with all its rewards and problems. From that day to the present, Princess Anne's public and private life has been on trial. Even during that first year, there was to be no allowance for youth or inexperience.

Not long after that eighteenth birthday, the Duke of Edinburgh revealed in a Grampian Television interview that the Monarchy

functions because occasionally you've got to stick your neck out. You can't just be wholly negative about this. I think if you feel strongly enough about it, and you feel that you are doing the right thing and that it is in the interest of people—sensible and intelligent people—you should go ahead and do it in spite of the fact that you may be criticised for it.

The idea that you don't do anything on the off chance you might be criticised, you'd end up like a cabbage and it's pointless. You've got to stick up for something you believe in.

Mindful of her father's words, Princess Anne began her public life. She was fully up to the challenge. Even then, she knew her own mind and insisted on her own way. Over the last two decades, with her forceful personality and no-nonsense attitude, it is she who has been partially responsible for pushing the monarchy forward along its evolutionary course.

At the beginning of that inaugural year, 1968, Princess Anne came over as a dumpy schoolgirl interested only in horses. She was decried by the fashion pundits on *Women's Wear Daily*:

Poor princess Anne. She's eighteen today and

41

nobody thinks she's a pretty girl. If I were her mother, the first thing I'd do is slim her down. The frumpy fur stoles, the middle-aged evening gowns. The overdone hair. The under-done hair. The sloppy grooming. It's about time Anne was allowed to bloom on her own.

Bloom, she did. By the end of the year, the press and public were extolling her. "Fantastic", said the public, "Princess Anne, the girl who is growing up the wittiest, gayest, and most natural of Royal Princesses" wrote the *Daily Mirror*, echoing the rest of Fleet Street. She was heralded the apotheosis of British youth, the example of monarchy as a trendsetter. All too soon, that splendid image was to be eroded. The stubborn temperament that set her apart as an individual (she has always been less decorous and more natural than other members of the Royal Family), turned her into the unacceptable face of Royalty. She refused to become a demure young princess available at any time "to add sugar to the life of the nation".

With her life ahead of her, there was no absolute necessity for Princess Anne to rush instantly on to the public platform, particularly as that was the only place for her to go. She did not share the options of her contemporaries, those lucky eighteen-year-olds on the threshold of wide open futures. They had the choice of going to university, of travel or plunging straight into a job, the start of their own "survival course" for life. For Princess Anne university was out; she dismissed it anyway as "a highly overrated pastime". Clearly hitching round the world was unthinkable. Although Dutch and Swedish princesses had been working for a decade, the idea of Princess Anne taking a job was totally untenable. Following a long tradition of the Royal Family, a short service commission in the WRENS, even the ATS was mooted, but never taken seriously. Instead, it was to be the public platform, but it was entirely up to her what she made of it.

For a start, the dumpy schoolgirl image had to go. Princess Anne lost weight simply by eating less, and, with her riding and active life, she has remained slim today as then. Another area where she felt that she was lacking was with her French. Her family were all linguists: Prince Philip is completely tri-lingual having lived and been schooled in Germany and France, the Queen's French is faultless and at that time, Prince Charles was learning Welsh for his Investiture as Prince of Wales. Princess Anne's French was adequate, but not brilliant. As a child, she had been tutored by Mlle. Suzanne Josseron, from the junior school of the Lycée in London, who even went to Balmoral in the late summer. When Princess Anne was eleven, she went with the Queen's former tutor, Mme.

Untermeyer, to France to stay with the Marquis de Saint-Genys at his château at Chapelle-sur-Oudon. For eight days, not a word of English was spoken. At Benenden, French was one of her "O" level subjects. To repair this schoolgirl French, Princess Anne went to the Berlitz School of Languages just off Oxford Street for a total immersion course. "It was a necessary evil and I wanted to get it over with," was how she described it. It is much to her credit that she applied herself to the course. After eight hours a day concentrated lessons over six weeks, she passed out of the school with good conversational French.

"There are plenty of occasions", Princess Anne, the veteran of thousands of public engagements, confided on Radio 4's *Tuesday Call* in 1985, "when you get a bit nervous, but equally I think if one didn't feel nervous about almost anything you probably wouldn't do it very well." She can only have been more than "a bit nervous" on her first solo engagement when she presented the leeks to the 1st Battalion Welsh Guards at their annual St. David's Day Parade, 1 March 1969. It is likely that she would have been even more nervous had not her father engineered the whole occasion. A great deal of care had gone into the planning of her debut, and it was no coincidence that the Queen's first solo engagement, aged sixteen, was to inspect her regiment, the Grenadier Guards, as their new

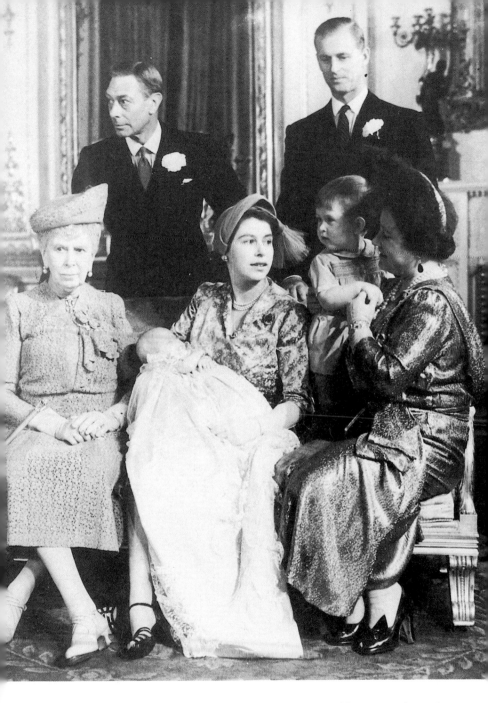

1. Four generations of the Royal Family together
for the christening of Princess Anne. October 1950

2. The reception committee for Queen Elizabeth the Queen Mother at Waterloo Station on her return from a tour of the U.S.A and Canada. Princess Anne waits patiently as the Queen talks to Sir Winston Churchill, November 1954.

3. Wearing a dress in the (polo) pony lines at Smith's Lawn in Windsor Great Park, May 1956.

4. Wearing the more usual form of dress at the Royal Windsor Horse Show, May 1955.

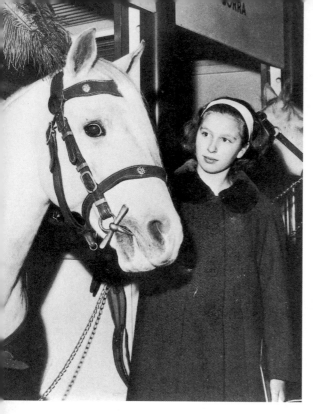

5. Behind the scenes at Bertram Mills Circus to see the horses.

6. Cowes Week August 1964. Princess Anne crewed on the Queen and the Duke of Edinburgh's Yacht Bloodhound

7. Princess Anne, right, as a soldier in the opera,
Dido and Aeneas, the Benenden School play in
the summer of 1968.

8. Princess Anne walks to the slopes at Val d'Isere with her instructor, Joel Usannaz, – her first skiing holiday, March 1969.

9. The 'Fashion Princess' – with Lady Susan Hussey
May 1969

10. Hats have always been a speciality of
Princess Anne's fashion sense.

11. Princess Anne is frequently in the company of the stars of stage and screen, as here, with Roger Moore of James Bond fame, November 1970.

Colonel-in-Chief. Virtually at the last minute, the Duke of Edinburgh who had agreed to present the Welsh emblem, found that he had arranged to be in two places at once, and so "passed on" the engagement to his daughter, leaving little time to reflect or for nerves. It was a thoughtful gesture as such fundamental mistakes simply do not happen in the Royal Household, especially Prince Philip's.

Nerves or no, Princess Anne carried out the engagement that bitterly cold day, with aplomb, to the delight of the regiment and the applause of the media. In a fit of exuberance, they praised her style, the way she handed out the leeks "like an old hand", they admired her green coat and mini skirt. Articles appeared on her jaunty cap. In return, Princess Anne enjoyed the limelight, for the first time directed solely on her, and the attention and publicity. Being "on show" suited her extrovert nature.

Other solo engagements followed that year, thirty in all. Each was carefully chosen, almost as if she were to sample one of everything on offer. The Queen lent her daughter one of her ladies-in-waiting, Lady Susan Hussey, an experienced courtier to see her through that "teething period". Typically, she launched a ship, the tanker SS *Northumbria* built on Tyneside; she attended the Cup Final at Wembley, where she found the noise of the hundred thousand fans, "somewhat astonishing". She visited factories. A

Rover owner herself, she toured the Rover car plant in Birmingham—a diplomatic choice with her mechanical bent and, as she puts it, her predilection for "anything that goes 'chug'". With her love of horses, she visited the new Equestrian Centre at Stoneleigh. She was seen (at separate times), driving a double-decker London bus and a police car at high speed on a skid pan, and a fifty-six ton Chieftain tank across rough ground. The tank was driven at Paderborn, West Germany, where she visited her regiment, the 14th/20th King's Hussars. The press reported how she had "elegantly" fired a Stirling sub-machine gun from the hip. "Even the best in the regiment could hardly do much better," enthused the instructor predictably.

The engagements were different enough to remain interesting, not too many to become boring, nor too few for her to be forgotten. Each one became a new challenge. From the beginning, Princess Anne wrote her own speeches, something she admits today as being "a chore, even if you know what you are talking about, although obviously it's easier if you do." Princess Anne had entered her public life, and the public could not see enough of her, or for that matter the rest of the Royal Family.

Where Princess Anne quickly adapted to her role in public life, it was the restrictions of her private life that were to prove more difficult. Everything about her was news. The arguments raged for weeks on the merits and demerits of not one, but two visits to *Hair*, the controversial musical. The show had caused a great furore when it first came out; it was the last play to be banned by the Lord Chamberlain. After her second visit, she joined the cast and some of the audience and danced on the stage, to the consternation of many. Princess Anne had much to contend with, not least the views of one senior Duke who wrote:

I was very surprised with her. She's not particularly pretty, yet she was wearing a trouser suit, of all things. I've seen the show myself. Dreadful. Dreadful. People doing all sorts of things under that blanket, and standing naked. I left after the first half. I don't know why they allow that sort of thing. Anne, of course, is very like the late Queen Mary. She'll go crazy and dance around. And suddenly she'll remember who she is.

At that stage in her life, Princess Anne at home was the odd-one-out of the Queen's children. Nine years senior to her next brother, Prince Andrew, and fourteen years older than Prince Edward, she "couldn't help being big sister with that sort of gap in age because you know that you always consider that they're not always getting the sort of discipline you got when you were small—so that is bad enough to start with."

Her brother was still somewhat distanced from her, up at Cambridge. At home, they lived in the same house, at opposite ends of the corridor, "—but that's all. He usually goes out at different times of the day." With their two younger brothers, they still kept the normal school holidays, when they saw "quite a lot of each other—then, roughly speaking, that's enough, quite frankly," as Princess Anne admitted on an interview for the children's programme *Blue Peter*. There, for the first time, she was torn between giving an honest answer to a straight question and not letting the family down. The "roughly speaking" and "normally speaking", to a certain extent, disguised the content.

For many children brought up together and as close in age as Prince Charles and Princess Anne, they would at least have some friends in common. However, the serious Prince of Wales gravitated towards an older set of friends, intellectual and sporting, with nothing in common with his sister. For his twenty-first birthday he chose Yehudi Menuhin and the Bath Festival Orchestra to play a Mozart violin concerto. His sister was more modern, as "trendy" as any girl her age. She had heard that the Royal College of Art had good parties with the best bands, but when she invited herself, she found that no one would dance with her, through fright or cussedness, so she had to be content with dancing with her detective.

If that was the sum total of Princess Anne's life, those early years would have been grim—few close friends, fenced in by Royal protocol and being watched at every minute outside the Palace portals. But Princess Anne had a world of her own where she found the friendship, the challenge, the escape. Hers was the world of the three-day event. The horse.

4

Hippomania

THERE are many elements that make up a champion: natural talent, opportunity, the right coaching and training, the will to win, and especially, a great deal of luck. When that champion is an equestrian, then those required elements are multiplied tenfold to accommodate the vagaries of the horse. Princess Anne is a champion; she possesses all those vital ingredients. She is an Olympiad; a champion of Europe. With her natural ability and opportunity, it would have been more surprising had she *not* succeeded. She was, after all, virtually "bred" to the position, horses being synonymous with the Royal Family—George VI maintained that his "sister Mary was a horse until she came out", while the Queen, as a very small child, announced that she, too, would "like to be a horse". However, it is not just the fact that she succeeded in a tough and competitive area, but that she succeeded so quickly and at the highest level that is to be so admired.

The questions put to Princess Anne by an invited audience at any radio or television programme are thoroughly predictable. Once

Save the Children Fund has been dealt with, and anything about her own children dismissed, out comes the ubiquitous question:

"Why is horse riding such a main feature in your life?" Princess Anne was asked on BBC2's *Open to Question* in 1984. She is now such an old hand at that type of programme that without a moment's reflection comes:

Generally, what dictates whether you are going for one sport or another is its availability to you personally; whether you live next door to a football stadium or running track or whatever may well influence the way you approach your own sport. I grew up with ponies. They, [and] horses, were always around. So, in logical terms it would have been daft to have gone off and started archery . . . I could have done, but I didn't, because they were there . . . and that's what I'd been doing longest, and felt I was best at.

Throughout her life, Princess Anne has been surrounded by horses—mews upon mews of them, stable upon stable. Horses were everywhere. There were the ceremonial coach horses in the Buckingham Palace Mews; even the post was picked up twice a day by a coachman driving a one-horse brougham. There were the Household Cavalry horses at Windsor Castle. Apart from her succession of ponies, there were her mother's hacks and her father's polo ponies stabled there too, the riding horses going to Sandringham and Balmoral on the Royal migration. Also at Sandringham was her mother's stud, at Balmoral the stalkers' ponies. There were horses in the nurseries, a rocking horse inherited from her mother which she rode for hours (some say the reason why the British upper-classes ride so well is that they begin on rocking horses).

The greatest single influence throughout Princess Anne's riding career has been her mother. The Queen is a horsewoman of international class. It is generally acknowledged that, had she been free to follow a competitive career, she could have reached the heights of her daughter. The Queen still rides four or five times a week, often one of her mother's retired steeplechasers. Her approach to riding is scientific; she has perfect control of her horse. Despite her diminutive size, she is strong; she is also very determined and quite without fear. When the Queen goes to a three-day event to watch her daughter compete, she is there not purely as a spectator but as an active participant reluctantly compelled to sit on the sideline. The Duke of Edinburgh was a good, but not top-class, polo-player. He had great striking power and an eye for the ball. More important, he had a special understanding of the science of the game, with all the brio and the determination to win. Although only an adequate horseman, he knew exactly how to obtain the maximum out of his ponies, interpreted by some critics as harshness. The qualities of both parents have come together in their daughter.

From the moment Princess Anne was first aware of the clatter of horses' hoofs, she has been immersed in family "equine competition". Her father played highly competitive polo throughout the summer. Her grandmother, Queen Elizabeth the Queen Mother, is a devotee of National Hunt racing, while her mother is addicted to the Flat, with an expert knowledge of bloodstock lines. The Queen was also involved in the highly competitive world of show jumping, lending her horse, Countryman, to the British team for the Stockholm Olympics in 1956. The team stayed at Windsor for their training. Princess Anne would not remember the European Horse Trials at Windsor in 1956, but, one of her earliest recollections must be the Windsor Horse Show, held annually in the Park. It was this rich blend of opportunity and spirit that took Princess Anne right to the top of her chosen sport.

That path to the top began at the age of two and a half with a shaggy Shetland pony called William, recalled as "a small hairy individual". William's main claim to fame was that he was so small that he was not noticed as a stowaway when he came over from Ireland. William was followed by a succession of ponies, a Welsh mare called Greensleeves, then Mayflower, then Bandit. If those ponies were unremarkable (Bandit, for instance, would only do one round of show jumping per day, steadfastly refusing to enter the ring for a second), Princess Anne's instruction was, and always has been, the best. After her mother's expert grounding, she was sent to the doyenne of all riding instructresses, Mrs. Sybil Smith, at Holyport near Windsor. If she was the best, she was also tedious: one of Princess Anne's earliest memories is of

One very large cob and two rather small grey ponies, all of them plaited and absolutely spotless from head to foot. Miss Sybil Smith was on the cob in the middle, Charles and I were on either side on the ponies. We were both on a leading-rein and we were *towed* around a cinder ring, but the fastest we ever went was a trot. I'm afraid I thought it was a grisly waste of time.

The other early influence on her riding was the Crown Equerry, Lieutenant-Colonel John Miller, who had himself ridden for Britain in the 1952 Olympic Games.

While the Queen and Prince Philip were careful not to spoil their children (the early ponies were shared), Princess Anne did have the great advantage that her love of horses and riding was indulged at every possible moment. As her pony was sent to Sandringham and Balmoral for all the relevant holidays, Easter was the only time for Pony Club activities. She joined the Garth Hunt Pony Club and competed on Bandit in her first hunter trial at Allanbay Park, Binfield, not far from Windsor. It was a taste of things to come. The venue was suitable; Allanbay is the home of Major and Mrs. John Wills, great friends of the Queen and Prince Philip (she is also the Queen's cousin), so that they could watch their daughter compete in comparative safety. The entry was declared late so as not to arouse undue interest, and consequently she went last in the running order. That day, she came second. One Royal perquisite was the gift of saddles from the County Borough of Walsall (the Mecca of saddlers), and bridles from the Loriner's Company (Princess Anne has been an Honorary Freeman of that City guild since 1972, as well as of the Worshipful Company of Farriers).

Bandit outgrown, Colonel Miller found a replacement called High Jinks. The 14.2–hand pony came from Ireland and was just the right choice. Only four years old, it had enough experience not to be dangerous, but needed a great deal of work to make it into a decent Pony Club hunter trialer. They pottered along together for a while, she recalled, "and then we did a few competitions. He was marvellous in every respect. . . ." Practically every week-end was spent at Windsor, and for Princess Anne the time was spent in the stables. She has always enjoyed the company of those who work with horses, and became equally at home sharing a mug of tea in the tack-room with the grooms as with her parents' guests in the drawing room. Riding also satisfied her need to be on her own, and she would take herself off for long rides in Windsor Great Park.

When she went away to school, Princess Anne's riding was restricted to the holidays. At their initial lunch at Windsor Castle, Miss Clarke, the headmistress of Benenden, stressed that they did "not encourage hippomaniacs", a remark which as Prince Philip had to explain to his daughter did not mean that "you are mad on hippos". However, she was allowed to stable High Jinks at the Moat House stables after her second term for a year. Once again, Princess Anne and her pony were back in the schooling ring, this time by another top name in the horse world, Mrs. Hatton-Hall. Both horse and rider benefited by the severe tuition, Princess Anne having according to her instructress, "one hundred per cent enthusiasm for riding and getting on with it; and she had excellent balance, sensitive hands and the courage and ambition to get on the back of any horse or pony in sight . . . if she was allowed to."

With the stable full wherever she went for her holidays, there was always a variety of horses to choose from—her father's polo ponies, various gift horses from abroad, her mother's riding horses. They were all different, some easy rides, some more difficult. "One splendid mare [was] . . . as solid as concrete from the neck backwards and she permanently ran away; one could pull for all one was worth but it made absolutely no impression. Luckily she always stopped before she got to a fence or a road, so it never used to worry one. I was really extraordinarily lucky with the ponies I had. They were by no means saints and they didn't do all the things they were told to do, but they taught me a tremendous amount." Later, on a trip to Austria, she had the fascinating experience of riding a Lipizzana stallion.

There is a world of difference between top-class Pony Club hunter trials and eventing, and, as Princess Anne admits, it was a step that was made for her, one that, left to her, she might not have made on her own. She would have "gone on hacking around quite amiably", she said, though she was beginning to feel that she'd like to do something else.

I'd have been quite happy (if I had been given the chance) to have had a shot at playing polo because it was something different and I'd watched it since the year dot and always enjoyed it; I think it is a very good game.

However, Colonel Miller sent his gelding, Purple Star, to the top-class eventer and trainer, Alison Oliver, at her stables at Brookfield Farm, Warfield for her to train for Princess Anne. "I was presented with Purple Star and more or less told to get on with it. There wasn't any conscious choice about it."

Colonel Miller had gauged it right. Purple Star was exactly the right horse. Well-bred and only five years old, he had great potential. Alison Oliver was also the right person to train Princess Anne. A top competitor herself, she is thoroughly professional, taking only pupils with talent as opposed to pupils who could just pay the fees. She is also direct and unintimidated, at least after the first two or three lessons. "If you're teaching somebody to ride, you have to fall into a relationship; in fact it is the easiest way of getting to know someone because you are on mutual ground." It is that "mutual ground" that Princess Anne so enjoys about that competitive horse world, where it is ability that counts, not breeding. For a start, at the stables all formalities were dropped, and Mrs. Oliver just called her Royal pupil "Anne". Today, Princess Anne counts her, and her husband, the show-jumper Alan Oliver, among her closest friends.

If Alison Oliver was the right instructress, then Princess Anne was the right pupil. She was calm, which is a good beginning as:

it meant that she was relaxed and that she didn't have any adverse affect on the horse. The most difficult people to train are those who are very stiff and rigid, because then you have to try and stop them doing something that they don't realise that they are doing. But Princess Anne was always very relaxed (and if anything, rather ineffectual) so there was something rather positive to build on, rather than something that one had to stop her doing. And she did have this natural balance and relaxation, which is so terribly important.

Once Princess Anne had decided that eventing was for her, she channelled all her energies into it. She could see many advantages in taking up the sport seriously. At that time, few people had even heard of a horse trial (it was not then televised), let alone been to one, so she could count on a certain amount of privacy. Compared to flat-racing or polo, eventing was fairly inexpensive. As there was no prize money to speak of, it was almost the last bastion of amateurism in the equestrian world practised by true sportsmen (even then, polo smacked of money and social advancement). She liked her fellow competitors, just as they warmed to her but, more important, it was an individual sport where if she excelled, it would be entirely through her own ability and nothing to do with anybody else. After all, as she has said, "when I'm approaching a water jump with dozens of photographers waiting for me to fall in, and hundreds of spectators wondering what's going to happen next, the horse is just about the only one who doesn't know I'm Royal".

Alison Oliver admitted that she had never had a pupil as dedicated as Princess Anne. If she had a public engagement, she would drive herself to the stables at dawn so as not to miss out on the day's training, or race down afterwards. She worked hard, and was worked hard. She never complained, or stood on her rank, doing any job that needed doing, however menial.

Her debut with Purple Star, a novice class for riders under twenty-one, came at the Eridge Horse Trials in Sussex in August 1968. She finished a creditable fifth out of thirty entries. Just as when the Prince of Wales had one ride in a steeplechase, he was asked when was he going to ride in the Grand National, so Alison Oliver was asked, after one ride, if her pupil would make it to the Olympics. She replied that "as things have gone so far she has done very well indeed. But I don't know whether it would be possible for her to develop into a rider of international class."

She had joined "the circuit". She travelled the country with Alison Oliver, who was no longer a competitor: "If I am riding myself, then I want to think only of my own worries, not anyone else's." Princess Anne was treated like any other competitor while actually competing, but she did have the advantage of staying in the house where the event was staged. They were always large house-parties, which gave Princess Anne the opportunity to meet and to make friends with the peers of her chosen sport. Equally, it gave them the chance to know her.

Princess Anne was lucky with Purple Star, and with her next novice horse, Royal Ocean. But it was the arrival of Doublet that really changed her riding career. There is one trait, almost a failing, in the Royal Family and that is that they do not spend enough money on their horses (except for Queen Elizabeth the Queen Mother who has never economised in that, or any, direction). The Queen's bloodlines at her stud are no longer top-flight, and this is reflected in her declining success on the flat. The Prince of Wales bought the wrong horse for himself when he started steeplechasing, refusing a far better horse because it was too expensive. He picks up some of his polo ponies from those bred at the Royal stud that do not make it to the race course. Of them all, Princess Anne was the most fortunate. The Duke of Edinburgh had high hopes of the colt out of one of his favourite polo ponies, an Argentine mare called Suerte, and an Argentine thoroughbred stallion, Doubtless II. Unfortunately for the Duke, Doublet, as it was named, grew too big (16.2 hands) for polo. His loss was Princess Anne's great gain and Doublet was sent to Alison Oliver to train and for her to event.

From the start, Doublet showed promise, winning the first time Princess Anne rode him in a novice hunter trial in the summer of 1969. Princess Anne found him

such a character. Although he was never a particularly easy passage, he had all that was required—he really could jump and he hated touching anything, he was very fast across country and, because he was such a frightfully conceited little horse, he did a very flashy dressage when he bothered to pay attention. It was only in his later days that he began stopping whenever he thought that he'd got himself seriously wrong—and he was undoubtedly the quickest stopper I'd ever come across. I disappeared over his head so frequently that people used to say to Alison: "Why is she riding that dangerous horse when she keeps falling off it?"

As Princess Anne moved slowly up the ladder, notching up wins and good places with her three horses, she was still just one of hundreds of young hopefuls with an eye to the top. Unlike the hundreds of young hopefuls, even the top riders then, she attracted the public and the press. When she started, those top equestrians indulged her as the keen and determined daughter of the Queen. When she started winning, they had considerably more respect for her. It was not long before they were chasing her. The Royal tour of Australia in 1970 where Princess Anne accompanied her parents bit into her riding schedule, but soon after her return, she and Doublet were back on the competition trail. They went well together, so successfully as to qualify for Badminton in 1971. It was a brave entry for one so comparatively inexperienced but, until horse and rider try it, there is no way of knowing what might happen.

Badminton is also very much a Royal occasion. The Duke of Beaufort invites most members of the Royal Family to stay for the four days and only in the most exceptional circumstances are the Queen and Prince Philip, the Queen Mother, Princess Margaret and her children not there. That year, they turned out in force, not mere spectators but related to one of the competitors.

Not only was Princess Anne competing over one of the toughest, and longest Badmintons, she was competing against the best of the European riders from Britain, Ireland, Holland, Switzerland and Sweden. Of the top British riders were Mary Gordon-Watson, the former World and European champion, on Cornishman, Richard Meade, Lorna Sutherland, Debbie West, Richard Walker and Mark Phillips on Great Ovation. After the first day, the dressage, Princess Anne and Doublet were in the lead with

Mark Phillips in second place. On the second day, she sailed through the roads and tracks and notched up a few time points on the steeplechase course. A downpour during the night produced a quagmire by the time Princess Anne started her cross-country section. As Alison Oliver remembered it:

> She rode the course in a way that I can only describe as innocent. There was a delight to her riding, which was fresh and enthusiastic, which is absolutely rare in competition at that level. She appeared to be enjoying herself all the way round and she was a joy to watch. Even though she was ambitious, even at that stage, there wasn't apparent the sometimes bitter single-mindedness that characterises so many of the world's leading sportsmen.

The "innocent" ended the second day in fourth place. At the show-jumping phase, Doublet put a foot in the water to drop her to fifth place. The winner was Mark Phillips on Great Ovation. By any standard, Princess Anne put up a remarkable performance at her first international event. It silenced her critics. It gave her great personal satisfaction as well as being a reward for all the hard work and faith of her trainer. The Queen was the intensely proud mother who had also bred the horse; the proud father also saw what the progeny of his favourite polo pony could do. Fifth place at Badminton won her £150 in prize money but more important, she was invited to compete as an individual at the European Championships to be held that year at Burghley.

The Eridge Horse Trials were considered the warm-up for the British competing at Burghley. While every other competitor was quietly preparing for the big event, Princess Anne was on an official Tour of Canada. On her return, just six weeks before the Eridge, she entered the King Edward VII hospital for an operation to remove an ovarian cyst. Everyone, including Alison Oliver, thought that that would put her out of the European Championships that year, but, having seen her in hospital, she found her "utterly determined to go ahead. I think," said Mrs. Oliver, "that it was then that I really appreciated the extent of her dedication and knew that she was made of the right stuff."

When she was finally released from hospital, Princess Anne showed exactly what she was made of. Riding had made her extremely fit, and that certainly helped her to recover faster. She went to a physiotherapist who gave her some exercises: she went to Balmoral, walking in the hills (in Scotland "the hill" is anything between one hundred and three thousand feet). After her twenty-first birthday on the Royal Yacht, she returned to Warfield just four days before the Eridge. It was pure guts that put her into the saddle there, and just two weeks later, took her to Burghley.

There can be few more beautiful settings in England than the park that surrounds Burghley House. It was laid out by Capability Brown: the European Championship course was built by Bill Thomson. When Alison Oliver and her Royal pupil walked the course, she noticed a "certain excitement" in her, "a challenge that might work out". The other competitors, who did not know her, were less sure. The other foreign competitors were unsure of her, "wondering if perhaps she was good enough to be in such exalted company." She was to prove them wrong. She had the horse; she had the skill; she had the luck and, most important of all, she had the spur tempered by the doubts of her critics that she should be there at all.

Luck and horse triumphed on the first day in the dressage: beautiful weather and a near-perfect performance from Doublet put Princess Anne in the lead. Dressage was one thing, but the speed, endurance and cross-country tests (seventeen miles in all, with nearly five miles and thirty-three solid fences) would certainly sort the "men from the boys". Again, Princess Anne would prove them wrong. She literally sailed round, enjoying the experience with only one slight hiccup at the water of the Trout Hatchery. Again it was that innocence that carried her through. She admitted, modestly, that "it was more my good luck than good judgement, because I hadn't the experience to know how fast I was going". On the last day, she had built up a near-unassailable lead as she went into the show-jumping ring. Scenting a Royal victory, crowds of nearly fifty thousand had come to watch: they, headed by the Queen and the Duke of Edinburgh, were not disappointed as Princess Anne and Doublet had a clear round. The Queen presented the new European Champion with the Raleigh Trophy and a cheque for £250. Britain also won the team event.

The effect of winning the European Championship was marked. She had been riding seriously for only three years, yet she had reached the top. Critics of her ability were silenced for good—even the Russian team thought her "an excellent rider and a wonderful girl" and asked their sports correspondent, Yuri Darakhvelidze, to present her with a bronze souvenir medal. The general public were initiated into a new and exciting sport (even the sub-editors of the sports pages learned not to call it show-jumping). Princess Anne was now even bigger news. She was voted Sports Personality of the Year by BBC viewers, polling four thousand votes more than the footballer George Best. Readers of the *Daily Express* also voted her Sportswoman of the Year. When she collected her trophy, she met the world motor-racing champion, Jackie Stewart, who was Sportsman of the Year. They have since become close friends. She also polled the highest votes from the British Sportswriters' Association for "the person who has done most to enhance British sporting prestige internationally".

There were, however, two sour notes to triumph. The saddest was that Doublet developed leg trouble, possibly at the Trout Hatchery, which was enough to put him out of the next Badminton and a possible Olympic place. The other was frivolous. The show-jumper and showman Harvey Smith claimed that Princess Anne was nowhere near Olympic standard and that anyway "any fourth-rate professional show-jumper entering her sport would clear the deck of every prize, in every event, every time." Champions came to defend Princess Anne and eventing. Richard Meade challenged him to ride round Badminton, but the challenge was never taken up and the remark was forgotten.

With Doublet still out of action, Princess Anne considered taking up the Badminton Committee's invitation to ride the Queen's horse, Columbus, but she declined. The big grey, known variously as the Monster or the Brute, was really too much to handle for a woman. When she defended her European title at Burghley, she withdrew half-way through the competition. Columbus needed a strong, male jockey and Princess Anne thought of Lieutenant

Mark Phillips for the job. "I didn't really know him at the time, but I thought that he was the most sympathetic of the good men I had seen riding. He's very, very strong (horses rarely stop with him and if they do, they wish they hadn't.") No one, least of all Princess Anne and Mark Phillips, ever thought that this partnership would lead to anything more than equine success.

The rift between Princess Anne and Harvey Smith cannot have been very deep as his partner, Trevor Banks, came up with what he thought was the right horse for her, a 16.2 brown gelding called Goodwill. Alison Oliver thought so too and the Queen bought him for her daughter. Although not ideal to begin with, Princess Anne schooled him to be ready in time for Badminton. Although she finished eighth, he had proved that he would be a useful second horse if, in defending her title, the faithful Doublet failed to qualify for the European Championships to be held at Kiev in the Soviet Union. Goodwill went. So did the press corps, for what turned out to be a field day, as before they left, Princess Anne and Mark Phillips announced their engagement. There was more in store for them. Goodwill had done an adequate dressage test and was all right on the steeplechase course. Before the cross-country, Princess Anne admitted to not feeling anything, "which is a bad sign and usually means something may go wrong". Something did go wrong: she took the second fence badly and she sailed over Goodwill's ears. She was in pain, her left leg was numb. Goodwill was stunned. There seemed no point in going on as if she withdrew, as an individual competitor, it would not affect the team result. Another of the many casualties at that fence, Janet Hodgson, staggered back on to her horse and completed the course. When the two performances were discussed in the press, Princess Anne came out of it badly, as they failed to make the distinction between an individual and a team entry. Where she held the respect and admiration of her fellow competitors, she once again took another fall with a biased press.

The Phillipses proved to be a formidable husband and wife team. They complement each other. For instance, if one had a problem with a horse, the other might be able to diagnose it. He helps his wife with dressage; she gives advice on cross-country. They have a friendly rivalry. If one had to be beaten, it would be best to be beaten by one's spouse. In fact, before their marriage, Mark Phillips was the one person whom she found the most difficult to beat. Just how good a team they were was seen after the first day of Badminton 1974. With two horses apiece, they were lying first, second, equal third with Goodwill at twenty-seventh. Anyone who knows anything about horses knows that the only thing that is predictable about them is that they are unpredictable. While Columbus steamed on to win and Goodwill improved to fifth place, the overnight leader, Doublet, was retired after a crashing fall. The horse that she had spent nearly three years hoping would find his old form, was out of the competition.

Not long after, Princess Anne and Alison Oliver were cantering across the polo grounds in Windsor Great Park when there was a sickening crack. It was Doublet's leg breaking. There was nothing to be done; he had to be put down. Princess Anne was distraught. One of the Queen's ladies-in-waiting, Lady Susan Hussey, said she "had never felt so sorry for anyone in my life. She was inconsolable and completely shattered." Even then, Princess Anne could not escape her critics who reported, erroneously, that two vets had examined Doublet and pronounced him unfit to ride, and the tears were of guilt.

At last, Princess Anne and Goodwill were chosen to represent her country, as opposed to being an individual entry, in an international tournament. She joined an all-female team for the 1975 European Championships, that year held at Luhmühlen. There were many who doubted womens' stamina over men and believed that eventing is too tough for them. Their allegations were disproved by the performance of the female team, or as the German press dubbed them the *"Britichen Amazonen"*, who clinched the team silver medal. Mary Gordon-Watson took the individual gold and Princess Anne, with a heavy cold, won a silver.

During the filming of BBC Television's documentary of Princess Anne in Kenya for *Blue Peter*, she let slip how much she wanted to ride in the Olympics. Her silver medal at Luhmühlen had made her and Goodwill possibles for the selectors for the 1976 Olympic Games to be held in Montreal. To every athlete, the Olympic Games must be the zenith of their aspirations. But, in her unassuming way, Princess Anne went one further when she said, "being on the shortlist I consider an achievement. If I get to Montreal I will consider that to be another achievement—and if I get a ride, then that will be quite something." She was selected, but not her husband, and she did get the ride.

Training began at Ascot. The press turned out in force and were very surprised to find a happy and united team. They left for Montreal, everyone travelling economy class which seemed to surprise everyone except the team members; the *chef d'équipe*, Colonel Bill Lithgow pointed out that "Her Royal Highness has never suggested being anything else but an ordinary team member—and neither have we." The organisers had no such qualms either, and she and Mark Phillips (the reserve member of the team) moved into Windsor Place, Bromont, the equestrian village, forty-four miles away from the main Olympic Village at Montreal.

The Queen (who had opened the Games), the Prince of Wales and his younger brothers, Princes Andrew and Edward, were all there, to watch her compete. But luck, that had so often favoured Princess Anne before, deserted her in Canada. On the first day, they were placed twenty-sixth after an unspectacular dressage. After her performance, half the spectators left the arena. The cross-country was a taxing course. Although none of the fences was particularly difficult, it was laid with a sand track, and the twists and sharp bends throughout upset the horses' natural rhythm. To make matters worse, overnight rain had made the going very heavy. Just before she was due to go, the gathering clouds finally broke and Princess Anne went off in a blinding rainstorm. The Queen, standing by the second fence, saw her daughter start well. At the seventeenth, everything went wrong. Goodwill hit a soft patch of ground on take-off and straddled the fence, throwing his rider to the ground. Dazed and still slightly concussed, Princess Anne remounted with an "I'm off. Give me a leg-up", and went on to finish the course seventeen fences later. Although the British team had been eliminated, she was, after all, still representing Britain. The arena filled up again to watch Princess Anne and Goodwill complete a rather slow, but clear, show-jumping round bringing her up to twenty-fourth place overall. When asked about her hopes for the next

Olympics, she replied, "It depends on whether I find another horse with as much ability as Goodwill."

To date, Princess Anne has not found another Goodwill nor had the same luck with her horses. Goodwill continued to give her more fun than success, as did another of the Queen's horses, Stevie B. The search to breed or find another Doublet or Goodwill is still on, but so far, not achieved. Even if such a horse is found, Princess Anne, with her massive work schedule today, could probably not afford the training time to achieve her former glory.

However, despite that punishing work-load, Princess Anne still finds the time for her novice and intermediate horses. She has also recently been introduced to a new and exciting equestrian interest—race riding. Her debut on the track came on St. George's Day 1985 at Epsom, at a meeting held specially for one of her favourite charities, the Riding for the Disabled Association.

For some time before the meeting, Princess Anne had been riding out at David Nicholson's stable. She had known of him for years, he having ridden steeplechases consistently for the Queen Mother, and is now a Gloucestershire neighbour. On the big day, 22 April, she was deputed to ride one of his big bay colts, Against the Grain, in the Worshipful Company of Farriers Invitation Private Sweepstakes. After she and her owner trainer had walked the course, a local trainer, Geoff Lewis who was in her party confirmed that, "she's one of the favourites. I know that she's worked hard at getting fit so she deserves to win. I couldn't keep up with her on foot." In the field of sixteen, there were many friends, like Virginia Holgate and Maureen Piggott, from the eventing world who had also "taken up the invitation". The race was over one and a half miles and run on the same course as the Derby. She started at odds of five to one, generous odds considering it was her first race and, on that course, it is experience that counts. After the race, she said she was immediately conscious that she did not come fast enough out of the stalls. However, three furlongs from home, she was level with No-U-Turn, but did not have the extra speed and finished a creditable fourth. Racing correspondents were generous with their praise of her performance, saying that the horse needed a longer race and that "she kept him clear of trouble and beautifully balanced throughout". Princess Anne enjoyed the experience greatly, but added, "You are not likely to see me in Royal colours." Apart from giving her a taste for race-riding, the race raised £32,000 from sponsorship and Sheikh Maktoum Al-Maktoum added a further £25,000.

Once bitten with the race-riding bug, it was very hard for Princess Anne to shake it off— particularly having the opportunity to work with racehorses in David Nicholson's stables so near. Race-goers at the September meeting at Goodwood were very surprised to see the name of the jockey left blank beside Little Sloop in the 3.35 race, being filled, just twenty minutes before the off, by "Princess Anne". "It was requested that the Princess's name was not put on the card because she wanted to be treated just like any other jockey", droned the racecourse spokesman. She started at eight to one, and, even when she was announced, "there was no rush to place bets on her but I think she has a lot of guts to ride". That day, Little Sloop finished sixth of seventeen runners. She was in the lead for part of the way then tailed off. Princess Anne's comment: "It was great fun"; her owner-trainer's comment: "the horse wasn't good enough". Next time out, at Redcar, she came in seventh. Then crowds at Chepstow Races, which included Peter Phillips, cheered Princess Anne as she came in sixth on French Onion, less than seven lengths behind the winner. The odds of twelve to one were generous, described by one bookmaker as "sympathy money". David Nicholson was pleased, describing it as a "highly satisfactory performance. She got left through no fault of her own but the idea was to drop in behind because that is the only way to learn to race-ride. She sat relaxed, didn't chase them up like a lunatic, made her effort in the straight and knew where she was going". Princess Anne's comment: "Highly delighted."

A good three-day event rider is perfectly capable of riding over steeplechase fences (Mark Phillips once rode round the Grand National course at Aintree on Columbus). David Nicholson confirmed that "Princess Anne comes here two or three times a week, and has been schooling horses for me over hurdles". She too thinks that she would be more suited to National Hunt racing. Elaine Mellor, the winning jockey of the Farriers' Race at Epsom, believes that "if she does decide to try, I'd say she has the courage and the experience". For one so very fit, there is still plenty of time to try.

Princess Anne has not always seen eye to eye with the general press, nor indeed the public (although one usually fuels the other). The sporting press, on the other hand, who generally know what they are talking about, have always been fair and loyal. They recognise talent when they see it, and there would not be many who would disagree with Jeffrey Bernard, who, when asked to contribute to Norman Parkinson's photographic book of women, wrote:

There are very few people who look more comfortable on a horse than Princess Anne. She looks, in fact, more comfortable in the saddle than most of us do in an armchair. She is positively indigenous to fetlocks, fences and falls. I remember once seeing her depicted on television sitting on the wrong side of the water jump, and she looked as much at home there, in that bleak bath, as she does when pictured with her husband, the captain, on a formal occasion and in a more Royal setting. Admittedly, she's no Piggott or Jonjo O'Neill, but the heart gets closer to the mouth when she jumps on her steeds than it does watching the professionals, simply because one fears for those Hanoverian bones. I fancy she'd rather stand on an Olympic plinth to be decorated with either Gold, Silver or Bronze than she would stand on ceremony.

Not that ceremony is, by any means, anathema; clearly this woman was born to terrify and there can be no question of her intuitive authority over her subjects human and objects equine. I'd like to see her name a horse Hyperion, look at it in the eye and dominate it from under her Fortnum's headscarf. In just about twenty-five years on the Turf I've seen processions of the best thoroughbreds winning the Derby and Ascot at its most Royal, but never have I seen anything so regally demanding as the jodhpur-clad thighs of Her Royal Highness hugging her willing, happy, happy steed.

Partisan yes, but a view shared by many who know her.

There is no doubt that Princess Anne has done much to make eventing a popular, spectator sport. With her involvement and success, it is an attractive proposition to sponsors, particularly to Range Rover who sponsor her husband. By the same token, eventing has done much for Princess Anne. At a time when the future looked bleak, when she did not know what to do after she left school, it gave a direction and some purpose to her life. It gave her a chance to prove to herself, and to her mother's subjects, what she is capable of. When her training programme was not going well, it taught her patience and humility: it even helped to curb that rich Hanoverian temper (on those occasions, Alison Oliver would send her to cool off in a horsebox). Eventing brought her world-wide fame (but not fortune); through her own efforts, she won admiration from the pony-crazed little girl to the hard-bitten journalist. It brought her real, and genuine friendship and, not least, a husband.

5

Love and Marriage . . .

WHEN citing the Duke of Edinburgh as a husband for the Queen, it has often been quoted that had he not existed, he would have had to have been invented. Although not in the same league as his father-in-law, the same might be said of Captain Mark Phillips. As the husband of Princess Anne, he is ideal. The Queen Mother, with her knack of coming up with exactly the right words, said: "They could almost have been computer-dated." That she fell in love with him was an added bonus.

Being so close in age, it would have been expected that Princess Anne and the Prince of Wales would have many friends in common, but Prince Charles's male friends tended to be that much older and more staid, with a passion for non-horse field sports and therefore of little interest to the younger sister. When she went away to Benenden, Princess Anne naturally went to the school dances, the boys being bussed in from the neighbouring public schools. They were heavily chaperoned. Miss Gee, her house-mistress, recalled that "once Princess Anne asked if she could go out with a boy who was a cousin of one of our girls and when I asked his name, she said she only knew his Christian name. So I had to tell her that I was certainly not giving her permission to go out with a boy whose surname she didn't know".

Having led a comparatively sheltered life, it would not have been unnatural if, like many before her and many to follow, she had "gone off the rails" when she left school. But Princess Anne was too intelligent for that course. She knew from watching her brother's progress that every man she was seen with, whether a chance aquaintance or a real friend, would be taken up by the press. She was affianced (in the press) to Prince Carl Gustav of Sweden on the strength of passing him a sandwich at a picnic at Balmoral aged fourteen. She also respected her parents too much to consciously embarrass them.

Although Princess Anne had a very sheltered home life, the picture of a lonely princess in a palace is totally false. She had her cousins. When she was eighteen, she went to stay at Barnwell with the Duke and Duchess of Gloucester for one of Prince Richard's parties. The Duchess believed that it "was her first party away from home and I doubt if she's been to another in the least like it". The party, held in a barn, was for the present Duke's Cambridge friends and lasted until dawn. Princess Alice was certainly wrong in her surmise. Also, members of the Royal Family rarely lunch or dine entirely *en famille*, there is always a representative of the Household or guests present. At Windsor and Balmoral they are joined by one or two of the officers on guard duty. Just as George VI provided for Princess Elizabeth what became known as "the Bodyguard", so the Queen and Prince Philip invited personable young men to stay. They were generally the sons of their friends, such as Lord Rupert Nevill's son, Guy, or Lord Halifax's son, Lord Irwin or Prince Philip's polo cronies. Neighbours' sons were invited too, as well as sons of the Household and bachelor serving officers from the Household Division. Such men went under the old-fashioned term of "escorts", but the press made no difference between them and boyfriends (in her first year after leaving school, journalists had romantically linked her with fourteen different men). Princess Anne most certainly did make the distinction.

The early front-runners in the Princess Anne Stakes—Andrew Parker-Bowles, Brian Alexander and Sandy Harper—had much in common. They were all very good-looking, well-bred, adequately well-off and active. Andrew Parker-Bowles, then a captain in the Household Cavalry, is the epitome of the dashing cavalry officer with autocratic good looks. A fixed-wing and helicopter pilot, he played polo for his regiment and distinguished himself in the 1969 Grand National by coming fourth on his horse, The Fossa. He later married Camilla Shand, a former girlfriend of the Prince of Wales. He is still a dedicated serving officer, and on his promotion to Lieutenant-Colonel, commanded the mounted regiment of the Household Cavalry at Knightsbridge Barracks. He now lives in Wiltshire, "within dining distance" of Princess Anne at Gatcombe. Parker-Bowles is still a frequent Royal visitor (he even has a corgi "By Appointment"), stemming from the time he escorted Princess Anne to the Royal Meeting at Ascot in 1970.

Some strange system of Royal protocol dictates that no single man can be invited twice to stay at Windsor Castle, so the Hon. Brian Alexander (a Royal neighbour, living at Winkfield, a few miles from Windsor) could not be asked again having stayed there three years before. Alexander, the son of the legendary Field Marshal Earl Alexander of Tunis, had everything (save a healthy bank balance) in his favour. With urbane manner, charm and classic, upper-class good looks (*Town and Country*, the American society magazine, almost changed their unalterable policy of having a woman on their front cover for him), he was popular and a much sought-after socialite. He is the archetypal courtier with impeccable manners. After a short service commission in the Irish Guards and a spell with the Rank Organisation, he joined Lord Glenconner, (then the Hon. Colin Tennant) in setting up Mustique, the rare and exclusive Carribean island resort. As managing director, he now lives there all the year round. An old Harrovian, he is a great friend of the Earl of Lichfield, and often stayed with Princess Anne at his house, Shugborough, in Staffordshire—she still holds the fastest time for a beginner on the monkey-bike course round park and garden. Not known for his interest or knowledge of horses, Brian Alexander was a keen club sports-car driver both on the British and European circuits. Of all Princess Anne's suitors at that time, it was thought that he led the field. Another of Lichfield's fast-living, "speed-merchant" set who took Princess Anne out was Piers Weld-Forester.

Both Parker-Bowles and Alexander were eleven years older than Princess Anne—they were thirty-one, she just twenty. Both were popular and had had many glamorous girlfriends before and after her. Neither is a snob, nor would wish to be with her just because she is the daughter of the Queen. Although Princess Anne had always lived in an adult environment, it is a measure of her maturity, humour and zest for the adventurous, that, even at the age of twenty, these two men found her so attractive.

Having spent a lifetime by the boards of the polo ground watching her father play, Princess Anne had many friends among the players. One was Sandy Harper who was, and still is, a keen player. Much closer to Princess Anne in age,

Harper was less traditional than Parker-Bowles and Alexander—it was he who took her to see *Hair*. Where they had escorted her to restaurants and smart dinner-parties, Harper took her to La Valbonne, the *avant garde* discotheque in Soho. A colourful character, he made good copy for the press with his relationship with Princess Anne. He is now married to the actress Suzie Kendall.

At the same time, Princess Anne had started eventing seriously, and with it came a new set of friends. One close friend was Richard Meade. Known as "Runnymeade" or "the Immaculate Conception" because of his well-groomed appearance, there was much in him that Princess Anne admired. While she was still in the novice section of the eventing world, he was at the top. A brilliant horseman, he was a double Olympic Gold Medalist and had won every major title in the eventing calendar. He too enjoyed her company: "Princess Anne has a very high sense of duty, but she has strong feelings about how much time she should devote to her private life and how much to her public life. She wants to enjoy both fully. She is humorous, amusing and very exciting to be with—but marriage. It's never discussed." Princess Anne devoted much of her private time to him.

Whatever their backgrounds, the disadvantages of taking out the Queen's daughter applied to them all—only Brian Alexander a great friend of Queen Beatrix of the Netherlands, was used to a life at Court. When Princess Anne was taken to a public place, a theatre, a restaurant, or even in the car, she was accompanied by her detective. He was always there, and however discreet he was, his presence can only have been dampening. Not that it could have been enforced, but under the Statute of Treasons (1351), having "carnal knowledge of the sovereign's daughter" was still one of the three capital offences (the other two were setting fire to a Naval dockyard and treason against the State). More of a threat was the constant attention of the press. Arranged Royal marriages were supposedly a thing of the past: Princess Anne was only half joking when she pronounced that "Princesses are getting a bit short in the market. I'll soon be next but they'll have a job marrying me off to someone I don't want. I'll marry the man I choose, no matter who he is or what he does". As with most things in her life, she has always had a very clear idea of what she wanted. As one friend said, "She was in the marvellous position of being able to play the field—in a subtle, Royal sort of way. But when she announces the name of the man she will marry, it will be someone nobody has ever heard of — not even us." The "friend" may not have been very loyal or discreet, nor was she entirely accurate. But the man who won through was, of course, Lieutenant Mark Phillips.

To all but the most ardent monarchist and serverest critics, Mark Phillips was a highly acceptable choice of husband for Princess Anne. To the public, theirs was a fairy-tale romance —"the handsome cavalry officer sweeps off the beautiful young princess" (something that *Private Eye* was to immortalise in *Love in the Saddle*, by Sylvy Krin). He was thoroughly English, with scarcely a trace of foreign blood, and thoroughly middle-class, which, although not by design, fitted in neatly with the new outward-looking Royal Family. He came from a long line of soldiers, mining engineers and bankers, with a maternal grandfather an aide-de-camp to George VI. One forebear was a miner, and there was a toe-hold in the aristocracy with an uncle, Major Joseph Phillips of the King's Dragoon Guards, who married Lady Katherine Fitzalan-Howard, daughter of the sixteenth Duke of Norfolk.

Although he was not perhaps the son-in-law that the Queen and Prince Philip would have immediately chosen for their daughter had arranged marriages still been the form, Mark Phillips did have many plus points. For a start, he made her very happy. With their steadfast belief in the benefits of a career in the Forces, he, as a professional soldier, was at least in the right job. Although initially shy, self-effacing and not over-inspiring, he was solidly dependable and unlikely to let the side down or embarrass them. He was a countryman at heart, and keen on all country pursuits, which certainly appealed to the Queen. His success with horses, in particular what he was doing with her horse, Columbus, weighed in his favour—there is a story that when the Queen was told of the engagement, she replied, "I shouldn't wonder if their children are four-legged."

Constitutionally, Mark Phillips was acceptable. With the Prince of Wales and two more brothers, there was absolutely no question of Princess Anne ever becoming Queen, so her husband would never become consort. There were also enough members of the Royal Family "to go round", so Princess Anne's husband was not needed as a supernumerary Royal. He was also fortunate in that there had been a precedent with both Princess Margaret and Princess Alexandra marrying commoners, although they had both been in Society and at Court for generations. Both had been able to continue with their careers, the Hon. Angus Ogilvy in the City and Lord Snowdon as a photographer.

Whatever Mark Phillips' advantages or disadvantages, or his appeal to others, it was, after all, Princess Anne who was marrying him. It is in her character not only to do what she wants in life, but also to get what she wants as well. Their initial common bond was, of course, horses, but the horse on its own is not enough to sustain a relationship. While he could always dominate her with his prowess in the saddle, he was also a good foil for her and her mercurial temperament, opposite poles attracting. Where she is quick-witted and forceful, he is calmer and slower; where she, by her presence and enthusiasm makes things happen, he just gets on with things in his own quiet way. He certainly has charm, but somewhat of a schoolboy humour.

After months of speculation, rumours became fact with the announcement in the Court Circular of 30 May 1973:

It is with the greatest pleasure that the Queen and the Duke of Edinburgh announce the betrothal of their beloved daughter The Princess Anne to Lieutenant Mark Phillips, The Queen's Dragoon Guards, son of Major and Mrs. Peter Phillips.

The courtship that led to that engagement was conducted on two levels: one by the protagonists, the other by the press. They played a game of cat and mouse, each using every trick to outwit the other. Of the two, the press was often the more accurate.

The announcement of their engagement came just five years after their initial meeting. Mark Phillips had been the reserve for the gold medal-winning British Equestrian Team in the Mexico Olympics. On their return, Whitbreads gave a reception in their cellars in the City, and Mark was asked to make up the numbers at a dinner-party at Buck's Club afterwards. The party was given by the Crown Equerry, Colonel Sir John Miller and included Princess Anne and the rest of the team. It was a memorable dinner, not least for Mark Phillips, who lost a contact lens half-way through the evening and spent the rest of the time in a blur. The two facts are not connected, but he is now an honorary member of Buck's Club.

Three years later, Princess Anne and Mark Phillips had become quite good friends, meeting frequently at various horse trials. In September 1970 she went to the Munich Olympics to support the British Three-Day Event Team, and danced most of the evening with Mark Phillips, at a party to celebrate the team and individual (Richard Meade) gold medals.

So casual was their friendship that when Mark Phillips once telephoned his mother,

> to ask if he could bring a girlfriend home for the week-end and she asked all the usual things: "Will you arrive in time for dinner?", "How long are you staying?", "What time are you leaving?" and was about to put the 'phone down when she asked, "What's her name?"
> When I said, "Princess Anne", there was a deathly pause at the other end of the 'phone. "You must be joking!" she stammered.

"No, I'm absolutely serious," I replied.
"When did you say you were coming?"
"It will take us an hour and a half to get there!"

After that Princess Anne often stayed at Great Somerford, but no one tipped off the press. They had about six weeks of comparative calm, protected by the loyal discretion of the village. "It wasn't until they went hunting together that the media latched on," said Mrs. Phillips. "Then all hell was let loose, and after that, they never had a moment's peace." As the Queen Mother remarked, when the news of her engagement finally broke, "When the cat is out of the bag, it is very difficult to stuff it back." For Princess Anne and Mark Phillips, the cat was certainly out of the bag and the chase was on. The press were certain that they were on to a winner of a story, even if the protagonists did not. They followed their hunting trips up and down the country; they "door-stepped" wherever they were staying; Great Somerford was permanently under siege. They took an added interest in all her official engagements. In a frenzy of excitement, they noted that Mark Phillips was staying for the weekend at Sandringham after Christmas, *and* was asked back for the next weekend; the French paper *France-Soir* had them "fox hunting, each carrying a gun". The result of weeks of cold watching, speculation and long waiting was finally worth it when she publically kissed him gently on the cheek as she said goodbye to him en route to join his regiment in Germany. She returned to Sandringham and greeted a lone photographer: "I'm on my own today. That's a pity isn't it?" Again *France-Soir* latched on to the story, although they were more convinced that "she was likely to become engaged to the horse rather than the rider" and that, "like her mother, she has a predilection for the company of horses, dogs and dukes in that strict order of precedence".

The press corps that covered Princess Anne's trip to Ethiopia in February 1973 was unusually large. As they strained with the heat, the flies and the discomfort in the bars of the hotels of Addis Ababa, they were rewarded with a statement from Princess Anne: "We are not engaged and there is no prospect of an engagement." Nor did they have much success with Mark: he said nothing and the regiment closed ranks. However, when she returned from Ethiopia, she sped past the turning to Windsor and her parents, and kept on down the M4 to Wiltshire where Mark, for the third time since he moved to Germany, was on leave. They returned to Windsor that afternoon, heading a large convoy of their followers. Despite the gas "go slow", a possible strike of Ford workers, a chronic situation in the coal mines and the threat of more unemployment with the steel industries' cutbacks, Arthur Lewis, Labour MP for West Ham North, still found time to question the Minister of State about the amount of leave Mark Phillips seemed to be taking. Said a spokesman for the Ministry of Defence: "We don't know. It is up to his commanding officer."

Their mutal love of horses and horse competitions naturally kept them in the open, and that meant in reach of the press and photographers. Mark Phillips, quizzed on their evasive tactics, admitted that "when two people are in love and want to be together, they find ways and means". So Princess Anne developed a series of decoys and disguises. She frequently left a horse trials in the back of a horse-box, with their horses. She later admitted that, "Only once, I don't quite know where I got it from, but I did own a wig at one stage" which she wore to meet her fiancé off the boat at Harwich. Mark Phillips

saw the car I was expecting, and, thinking I shouldn't hang about too much with all the press around, chucked my cases in the back of the car and jumped into the passenger seat —and there was this strange girl. My God, I've got into the wrong car!

When Princess Anne was seen riding Mark Phillips' new horse, Persian Holiday, surely that was an engagement present and tantamount to a betrothal. Instead, a vehement denial came from

Princess Anne. She was jumping her horse, Flame, at Warfield when she spied a reporter and photographer watching her from a footpath. Cantering over to them, she tackled Gillian Garner, an agency reporter. An exchange followed:

Princess Anne: Haven't you ever seen anyone train horses before?

Garner: Yes, on many occasions.

Princess Anne: Did you ask anyone to confirm that it is a public footpath?

Garner: No, I did not. But if I were asked to go, I would remove myself.

Princess Anne: Well, I might remove you. Which paper do you work for?

Garner: I work for an agency serving the nationals.

Princess Anne: Well that sounds as if you are being deliberately evasive. What's the name of the agency?

Garner: The Southern News Service, which represents the national dailies.

Princess Anne: Thank you. I don't know what you people are doing here every day.

Garner: With respect, surely you must be aware of the speculation and rumour and romance between yourself and Lieutenant Phillips?

Princess Anne: There is no romance between us and there are no grounds for these rumours of a romance between us. We are finding it difficult to train properly with so many press photographers surrounding us all the time. I can't understand why there has been all this interest in us riding together. Lieutenant Phillips has been coming here solely to exercise the horse he is riding at Badminton which is stabled here and belongs to the Queen.

The conversation was terminated by the arrival of her detective. Buckingham Palace Press Office issued the usual denial: "If Princess Anne has said this, perhaps Fleet Street will believe her and let the Princess and Lieutenant Phillips train their horses alone in peace."

But they were not to be left alone. Three days later, a lighted crow-scarer was lobbed over the wall at the ever-attendant photographers and reporters outside the Phillips's house at Great Somerford. No one was hurt and no one owned up. Major Phillips dismissed it with, "There is nothing I can do about it now. It doesn't worry me very much".

The more Princess Anne and Mark Phillips kept reading in the press that they were on the point of becoming engaged, the more they were determined not to. Whatever their feelings for each other at that time, it can not have helped having the press analysing what was, or what was not, there. Anyway, they had more important things to think about—Badminton. As Princess Anne admitted later:

> Mark never mentioned any idea of getting married and I definitely got the impression that he thoroughly enjoyed his bachelor existence. Anyway, even if I thought there was anything really serious going on at the time, I don't think either of us would have been in the least bit intelligent if we'd decided [to get engaged] before going to something like Badminton because we were, after all, competitors in the same sport, and I think that it would be tantamount to irresponsibility because we might have been totally non-speaks by the end of it. Even if he had asked me I would have said, "Don't be ridiculous—this might be a disaster".

But Badminton was not a success for either of them. Mark Phillips was bidding for a record third win on Great Ovation. That horse was retired lame, and two falls from Columbus put him out of the running. Princess Anne had finished a disappointing eighth on Goodwill. On that Sunday evening, they went for a walk across the farm, feeling somewhat downhearted. They found great consolation in each other and, literally on the spur of the moment, he proposed to her. Princess Anne confirmed this cavalier approach when she said that she thought that it

96

"was the first time he'd thought of it". She had thought of it and, if the proposal was to be made, she would accept, which, of course, she did. For once, she was pre-empted by the press.

The Duke of Edinburgh, recently returned from a five-week tour of nine countries and therefore out of touch with the situation, can only have been surprised at the request of the petrified, tongue-tied lieutenant to marry his daughter. Mark Phillips survived the ordeal, the Duke "being very good" to him. There was to be a delay of a further five weeks while members of the family, the Prime Minister, Heads of State, Commonwealth leaders were all informed of the engagement before the news was made public.

The official announcement of the engagement was carefully stage-managed. All the signs were there for those who could recognise them. Most members of the Royal Family had congregated at Craigowan, a house on the Balmoral estate kept as an overspill for Household or for short visits of the Royal Family when they do not wish to open up the Castle. Princess Margaret and her children were staying with the Queen Mother at Birkhall nearby. The Prince of Wales had flown back from his ship in St. Kitts just for the weekend. Finally, the engagement was made public on the Tuesday evening and everyone concerned heaved a sigh of relief.

At first the press were annoyed as they

believed that they had been let down by the Buckingham Palace Press Office. They simply could not, and would not believe that the denials of an imminent engagement were not true. However, their fire was short-lived. At that time, the country was labouring under the worst economic crisis for decades. There were scandals; the Poulson affair, Lord Lambton and Lord Jellico with their call-girls and the antics of Bernie Cornfeld. Abroad, the United States were gripped by Watergate. Just when the country is in the grip of some crisis, the Royal Family can almost be guaranteed to come up with something to brighten the scene. The Victorian historian, Walter Bagehot, forsaw it all when he wrote,

> All but a few cynics like to see a pretty novel touching for a moment the dry scenes of the grave world. A princely marriage is the brilliant edition of a universal fact, and as such, it rivets mankind. . . . Just so, a royal family sweetens politics by the seasonable edition of a nice and pretty event.

The engagement did just that. Here, at last, was popular news that could be heralded around the world. At least it made one American matron happy. Preparing for a garden party at the British Embassy, she was thankful for "Anne and her marvellous timing. It would have been a bit tricky chatting to all those Englishmen about those dreadful lords and that call-girl business. But now we'll just talk about that wonderful little girl and that lovely man of hers."

From the moment the engagement was announced, Princess Anne was a heroine; she could do no wrong in the eyes of the public or the press, her past sins were forgiven. They cheered her on her way to Buckingham Palace, they marvelled at her when they were photographed and filmed on the lawns. For the first time, they saw her fiancé out of uniform and not doing daring things on a horse. They warmed to them both, and their his and hers black labradors, Moriarty and Flora. They loved the way they involuntarily held hands as they crossed the lawns, but not so tightly that the engagement ring could not be seen—one that she had chosen from a selection brought round by Garrards within keeping of the fortunes of an Army captain. But when, with disarming honesty, Mark Phillips admitted that he had not thought of what marrying the Queen's daughter would do to his life, saying, "If that thought had stopped me marrying the person I loved it wouldn't have been much of a relationship—we both loved each other", it was enough for the British public, indeed for the rest of the world. That, unlike the Earl of Snowdon, he supposedly declined a title gave him the final seal of approval.

"I'd prefer a quiet wedding," Princess Anne

is reputed to have said, "but the Queen wants Westminster Abbey." So they were married in Westminster Abbey, on 14 November 1973, Prince Charles's birthday (and that of the Archbishop of Canterbury, Dr. Ramsay, who married them). A Royal wedding is a unique affair. It is something the British do supremely well, making a public spectacle out of a private occasion, giving a very real sense of sharing it with anybody who wants to join in—a triumph of love over show business. It invariably floors the sceptics, gives great pleasure to millions, financial profit to some, and exhausts all who are even remotely part of it. A Royal wedding is the culmination of months of hard work and frayed nerves; the co-ordination of the thousands, both directly and indirectly working towards the same end. For every one of those involved with the ceremony and family, there are a hundred on the periphery: the massed, twittering media, the manufacturers of thousands of souvenirs and the producers of articles and books and the miles of deep genealogical research.

The actual mechanics of the wedding devolved on the Lord Chamberlain, Lord Maclean, head of the Queen's Household and his staff of twenty-five. "Strictly speaking," he pronounced, "the wedding is a private affair although there will be the trappings of State." The guest list was whittled down to 1,600 (three extra staff were employed just to write out their invitations) and that included twenty-five members of foreign royal families. The Queen's first cousin, the twice-married Earl of Harewood was not asked: "Anyone who is a guilty party or a co-respondent in a divorce," decreed the Lord Chamberlain, "is not received socially at Court."

Extra staff were brought in to deal with the flood of presents, solicited and unsolicited. The official announcement that "she needs just about everything. She has hardly a thing to start with, and is building up from scratch", was taken literally, and thousands of household items flooded in (Princess Margaretha sent eight dozen coat-hangers). Some were original: the Nottinghamshire County Council donated her the number plate 1 ANN; others welcome—the Army raised £4,600 for a Queen Anne chest of drawers, (Willie Hamilton, the anti-monarchist MP was quick to point out that each soldier was indented for 5p, each officer 30p unless they "contracted out" within forty-eight hours in writing). Each present was entered in a book, (101 pages) and duly thanked for by letter by one of the staff. Those presents that were thought unsuitable were returned. After the wedding, a selection went on view at St. James's Palace, the entrance money of 25 pence going to various charities. Her own family were generous with jewellery, furniture, carpets and porcelain, the Prince of Wales adding a pair of leather slips for his future brother-in-law's pair of guns.

Westminster Abbey was closed for nine days. In a fever of excitement, seventy people from the Dean to the carpenters "worked to capacity" to make sure all went well. Pale gold spotlights were installed to flatter Princess Anne's complexion. Camera positions were worked out and stands made to accommodate them. This wedding was to do for colour television what the Coronation did for black and white—television manufacturers went on full production, sales and rentals rocketed. Souvenirs of every conceivable (and inconceivable) form flooded on to the market: "Anne and Mark" mania spread from the Bond Street jewellers with gold and silver to the Oxford Street touts selling Taiwan tat.

To keep the tempo going, Buckingham Palace let out the occasional announcements: "Princess Anne has decided to have only two attendants and no senior bridesmaids, because she wants the wedding to be as simple as possible for the only daughter of a sovereign". Instead, she had her nine-year-old brother, Prince Edward and first cousin, Lady Sarah Armstrong-Jones. The groomsman, Royal parlance for the best man, was announced as the Army discus-throwing, hurdling and bobsleighing Captain Eric Grounds, adjutant of the Queen's Dragoon Guards, aged twenty-five and height six foot four inches. A special full dress uniform had to be invented for the Queen's Dragoon Guards. The designer came up with a scarlet and gold tunic, with blue velvet collar and cuffs and blue piping down the front edges. Three ill-fitting uniforms were made, one each for the groom and his man, and one for Madame Tussaud's, at a cost of £250 each. Other details were kept a secret—what Maureen Baker of Susan Small and her team of fifteen had dreamed up for the wedding dress (at least until eight o'clock on the wedding morning so that by lunchtime copies were already available.)

There is no reception after a Royal Wedding, so those friends who were not asked to the Abbey were invited to a ball at Buckingham Palace the week before (also organised by the Lord Chamberlain). Mark Phillips' stag-party on the Monday night at Julie's Restaurant caused a stir with the neighbours, and in the press: "I drank champagne until it was coming out of my ears," he recalled. It seemed that he could be forgiven anything, even his performance on television screened the night before the wedding.

From the moment the engagement was made official, Mark Phillips was given a crash course in Royal behaviour in six months. The Army released him to accompany Princess Anne on formal and semi-formal occasions, and to ride his horses. This caused a certain amount of adverse comment. An article appeared, amazingly, in the *Sunday Express* asking who "pays Corporal Johnson when he goes to the Phillips family farm for weeks on end, lives in digs and looks after the horses? We should be given an answer to that. We should also be given a straight answer to the question of why a man who is a qualified and expert Chieftain tank driver should be wasting his time playing around with horses." The Army also brought in one of their former instructors to train him how to conduct himself on television: the instructor unkindly, told him "to keep quiet and keep smiling". Unfortunately the interview was not a success: so polished was Princess Anne's performance (even against the strains of the band outside) that it made her fiancé's stammerings and hesitations appear worse than they really were. However, he did make one good point:

I think also that the intense interest which the press and television have shown in the wedding, and the people all over the world who would appear to be interested in the wedding, reflect a little bit on the state of the world at the moment, in that every day people pick up the paper and read about some disaster or some new scandal, and I think they are really rather relieved to read about something that is genuinely happy and good.

At least he and Walter Bagehot had something in common. Those watching were intrigued to hear that they both used the third person, something parodied later in the popular television

104

series *Till Death Us Do Part*. In one episode, Alf Garnet's daughter inquired, "Is one going to one's pub?"

On the day, hundreds of thousands of people lined the route that sunny November morning from Buckingham Palace to Westminster Abbey (some had even spent the night there). Hundreds of millions more around the world watched the live television coverage, others heard the radio coverage that began long before dawn. Every aspect of the couple and the day was covered— astrologers made predictions; genealogists explained that they were, after all, "related" (thirteenth cousins three times removed). Finally, on cue, the bride appeared in the Glass Coach with her father for the fifteen-minute journey to the Abbey. Trumpeters from the groom's regiment played a fanfare composed by the Master of the Queen's Music, Sir Arthur Bliss.

Cameras within the Abbey showed every step of the happy bride's procession as she walked up the aisle, accompanied by the Archbishop of Canterbury, her godfather, the Reverend the Hon. Andrew Elphinstone and senior clerics and their vergers. She looked happy and relaxed, which, according to lip-reading experts hired to pick up those private asides she was: when Prince Philip asked her if she were nervous, she just smiled and replied, "No, of course not." The wedding service itself was kept as "private" as anything can be with five hundred million viewers, but there were no cameras in the Sanctuary where they were actually married, nor in the Chapel of Edward the Confessor where they signed the register. At the end, husband and wife, after a deep curtsey and bow to the Queen, processed down the aisle to Widor's "Toccata". The commentators were pleased to point out that Princess Anne had first heard it when aged eleven, as bridesmaid to the Duke and Duchess of Kent. The lip-readers could also point out that she kept up a steady conversation with her husband. In between asking him if he was all right and to prepare to wave to the crowd on the way home, she whispered by the doors, "What now? Are we going home!?"

The procession "home" was cheered all the way. In the open landau they even noticed, and smiled at, a banner in the crowd from the Royal Veterinary College: "It's too late to say neigh!" Then came the balcony appearance at the stroke of half-past one. The Mall was packed. The cheering went on and on. Not unnaturally, Mark Phillips was totally overawed by it all. He admitted that he "just couldn't believe that so many people wanted to wish us well, and had gone to so much trouble to show pleasure in our happiness. It wasn't as if I had really done anything to deserve it—but it says so much for the Royal Family and Princess Anne that they wanted to be there." The wedding breakfast followed, after which Prince Philip made the first speech: "Unaccustomed as I am", a long pause, "to speaking at breakfast . . ."

The crowds were still there and cheered them when they left for the first leg of their honeymoon (they changed their landau for a car at the Royal Hospital, Chelsea) and drove to Thatched House Lodge in Richmond Park which Princess Alexandra and Hon. Angus Ogilvy had lent them for the night. The street-parties continued and the television and radio relived each moment of the day until closedown. The next day, they drove to Heathrow and boarded the British Airways flight for Barbados to join HMY *Britannia*. The Royal Yacht conveniently only had to make a slight detour on its way to New Zealand to accommodate the honeymoon cruise round the Windward Islands, West Indies. Once again, the press played a cat-and-mouse game with the Royal Yacht. That fortnight, Princess Margaret was moving into her house on Mustique and it was thought that they might go there. Dozens of bookings, all in the name of Smith, were requested and refused at the Cotton House Hotel: charter planes landed on the airstrip filled with photographers only to be politely refused entry by the Hon. Colin Tennant (the present Lord Glenconner). When the Royal Yacht did arrive, Princess Anne and Mark Phillips just visited the wreck of the burnt-out French liner, the *Antilles*, half a mile from the

107

shore but did not come ashore. For the rest of the cruise, the honeymooners were marooned in the morning on a deserted island while the Royal Yacht drew off the press corps, then she picked them up at dusk. The cruise ended on the Galapagos Islands and they had to "work their way home" with a two-week official tour of Equador, Columbia and the West Indies. They returned from sun and warmth to a grey and cold December in time to travel to Windsor for Christmas and a new life as husband and wife.

At home, Britain basked in the reflected glory of the wedding. There were naturally a few critics who sniped at the lavish expenditure at a time of economic hardship: "I just hope", a non-political woman from Rye wrote with some bitterness, "the pensioners found their bread and cheese a little more palatable from watching it, the homeless and jobless a little warmer and a little more wanted, the assembly-operative a little more content with his work." In fact, the wedding cost the British tax-payer very little. The wedding was a totally private affair, paid for, as is usual, by the bride's family (in this case, by the bride's mother). The only bills the Government picked up were the overtime for the police, transporting soldiers to line the route and special stands erected by the Ministry of the Environment.

12. A boys' centre, Nairobi 1971.

13. A present from the Shah of Persia, a two-year-old colt named Awtash. January 1972.

14. A three-day safari to the Simeon Mountains, Ethiopia February 1973.

15. Princess Anne's engagement to Lieutenant Mark Phillips, May 1973.

16. An official wedding photograph by
Norman Parkinson, taken in the Long Gallery,
Windsor Castle. The dress is by Zandra Rhodes.
October 1973.

17. Despite a world-wide audience of 500 million viewers, the wedding of Princess Anne and Captain Mark Phillips was still a family occasion, Westminster Abbey, November 1973.

18. Colonel-in-Chief of the 14th/20th Kings Hussars, preparing to drive a Chieftain tank, Germany 1970.

19. Princess Anne presents the Carl-Alan Awards, 1975.

20. Princess Anne and her husband, riding out
before the Badminton Horse Trials, April 1975.

21. Gatcombe Park, Gloucestershire, the home of Princess Anne and Mark Phillips. The addition of the conservatory makes the house appear much larger than it really is.

22. Earl Mountbatten, greets his great-niece at the Albert Hall, May 1977.

23. Princess Anne's first born, Peter, December 1977

6

Occupational Hazards

"WHEN you're married," Princess Anne told her husband's biographer, Angela Rippon, "you are not living on your own. You're living with another person, and you have to adapt to some degree. It's the same when you have children, the whole structure of your life changes. . . . Really, if you didn't change as you went along you'd be a bit of a disaster; that's what life is all about really—adapting to experiences." By her own admission, there were problems in their first two years of marriage, but "they are not the same kind, I'd have thought, that many couples of our age have".

For those first two years of their marriage, Princess Anne and Captain Mark Phillips lived at Oak Grove House, within the grounds of the Royal Military Academy, Sandhurst, where he had been appointed an instructor. As a serving officer and successful rider, he posed something of a problem. Nothing would have suited him better than to continue soldiering with his regiment in Germany, but clearly that was impossible. There was no parallel with Princess

Elizabeth either when she married and joined her husband serving in Malta. There she had a house commensurate with her position while in Germany there was nothing remotely suitable among the married quarters for Princess Anne. For Princess Elizabeth, there were not the public demands now made upon the younger members of the Royal Family. Also the regiment had a job to do as part of the NATO forces which they would certainly not have been able to discharge properly had they been continually worrying about the Royal wife of one of their junior captains. If, as Willie Hamilton had expressed it, he could not drive Chieftain tanks, at least he should be able to ride horses. To send Mark Phillips to a desk job in the Ministry of Defence in Whitehall would have hampered his riding career, so Sandhurst, with its university terms and holidays, was ideal. There was also a house for them to go with the job.

The post-Christmas holiday of 1973 lasted until the middle of January at Sandringham, then Princess Anne and her husband joined the Queen on the Royal Tour of Australia, New Zealand and the Pacific Islands. The Tour was an admirable chance for Mark Phillips to see first-hand how "the job" was done by two professionals, and also a further chance for the Queen to know her new ADC better.

By the time they returned, Oak Grove House was ready for them to move into. Oak Grove is a late Georgian, five-bedroomed house built at the same time as the rest of the Military College. Normally it is occupied by some senior member of the staff, but when Princess Anne was looking for a house, it was vacant and the one that suited her best. A captain's married quarter would not have been practical for the sovereign's daughter. Much was made of the fact that, with the mortgage rate rising to 11% and the shortage of council housing, the Phillipses should only be charged £400 a year (the tabloids translated it as £8 per week) and have £25,000 spent on it. In fact, the Department of the Environment spent £5,000 on essential repairs, which they would have done, whoever the tenant, in the four-year maintenance cycle for Army married quarters. Likewise, the rent was subsidised as a normal service tenancy. Princess Anne paid the estimated £25,000 for what the American Ambassador, Walter Annenberg, described as "elements of refurbishing rehabilitation" which included a new garage and wallpaper supplied by Buckingham Palace.

This "element of refurbishment" (a favourite line of the Royal Family's) was carried out to Princess Anne's and her husband's orders. The exhibition of their wedding presents at St. James's over, their first house was well and comfortably furnished. As their first home, it was ideal. Captain Phillips was right on his job, a short stroll from the main college. It was well placed for Princess Anne, being only fifty miles from her office in London—she kept her suite at Buckingham Palace, as she does today, to store her "working clothes" and for those nights when she cannot drive home after an evening engagement. Windsor was even nearer. There were also six good boxes for their horses close to Alison Oliver at Warfield where Columbus was still stabled. The one major draw-back to the house was that it was close to the road and open to possible attack. As at Sandhurst itself, there was a constant and very real threat of IRA bombings at nearby Aldershot, "the Home of the British Army". However, the local police built a command post inside the gates and raised the perimeter fence by two feet. Floodlights were installed round the house. Fortunately, these precautions worked.

During the first two years of their marriage spent at Sandhurst, it was easier for Princess Anne to adapt to being a wife, than for her husband to adapt to being married to a member of the Royal Family. Those early problems were not of their making, and any one was enough to put a strain on any new marriage. Mark Phillips was wearing three hats. He had a full-time job in the Army, he was a top three-day event competitor with all its time-consuming training, and he was consort to his Royal wife as well as being the master of his own house. Because of their differing lifestyles, they did not spend enough time together. He once complained that:

I am away on Army exercises or she's away. A few months ago [at the end of 1976] we never seemed to be at home together. We sort of met in passing. I would be working all day and maybe have to go and do something in London and get back very late at night and I would be off again early next morning. Sometimes we feel very tired fitting in all our commitments. We certainly don't spend as much time together as we would like.

Add to that, Mark Phillips admits that when he is tired (or wasting on a diet) his temper is short. He admitted that he found official visits tiring and hated standing around for hours. In those early days when he accompanied Princess Anne on some of her engagements, she sometimes found it difficult having him "tagging along at functions and things". Again, it is the house monitor syndrome from her schooldays when, being so good herself at her job, she could not see how others could not grasp the situation and shine like her. Then Princess Anne is a real professional, throwing herself into her role. After an official tour, it took her days to unwind: "I come home and drive everyone nuts because I natter—sometimes for a day or two—before I gradually wind down."

While not unhappy with her lot, Princess Anne found it difficult to evaluate those initial two years of her marriage, not having much of a yardstick to go on. She admitted that they did not

> come into contact with many other young marrieds the way other people do. There are one or two couples here either one or other of us have known previously but very few. Most of my friends—girls I was at school with—are married and living in London, or Scotland or scattered about so there isn't much chance of comparison.

One of their friends was Malcolm McVittie, a junior subaltern in the Argyll and Sutherland Highlanders, whom Anne had met when his regiment mounted the Royal Guard at Balmoral. Scottish foot regiments take it in turn to mount the guard and, during the time the Royal Family are in residence, each of the officers dine there, and at the Queen Mother's residence, Birkhall, several times throughout the tour. The regiment also invites the whole Royal Family back for a drinks party, occasionally, as in the case of Princess Anne, to dine in the mess. By chance, McVittie was also posted to Sandhurst at the same time, and was the only friendly face she knew. Later, she was to become sponsor (Royal parlance for a godparent) to their daughter, thoughtfully named Alice Louise. Apart from these "one or two friends" there were plenty of acquaintances, whom they saw and entertained on a totally informal basis.

Despite the irregular pattern of their lives, and the tremendous hard work that they put into their jobs and their horses, a form of routine did develop. Every word, generally trivia, that filtered out of Oak Grove was eagerly devoured. It was learned that they did manage to breakfast together, although Princess Anne did not talk ("more like grunting than chatting"); that they both rode out early and Mark Phillips would snatch a half-hour over lunch to take out another horse and that they watched *Kojak* and *Match of the Day* on television on Saturday nights, when of course they were not holding those "informal dinner parties for the junior officers and their wives and girlfriends" where her favourite place was sitting on the floor.

Then quite the most appalling event of the whole of Princess Anne's life occurred just eighteen weeks after her marriage. Ian Ball, a man with a history of mental illness tried to kidnap her in what is now referred to as the Mall Incident at half-past seven on 24 March 1974. Princess Anne and Mark Phillips had been to a private viewing of a short film, *Riding for Freedom*, showing the work of one of her special charities, Riding for the Disabled. They left Sudbury House in the City of London, with her lady-in-waiting, Rowena Brassey (now Mrs. Andrew Feilden) and detective, Inspector Beaton, and drove back to Buckingham Palace, before going on to a private dinner-party. Their chauffeur-driven limousine cruised gently round Trafalgar Square, under Admiralty Arch and down the Mall. They had just passed the turning to Clarence House and St. James's Palace and in sight of the Victoria Memorial and the Palace when a white Ford Escort accelerated past them, then swerved in front of their car. The chauffeur, Alexander Callendar, a Scotsman who had been in Royal service for twenty years, pulled up sharply. It was quite dark.

At that time, they all thought it was no more than a "Bolshie motorist". Inspector Beaton got out of the car to investigate, and, as Princess Anne recalled:

> when he came round to the back of the car, he realised that the man had a gun. The policeman [Beaton] got off one shot which I am convinced came through the back window of the car as something hit me on the back of the head—so I thought that was a good start.

In fact, the inspector had been shot in the chest. His gun had jammed so could not fire again but fell to the red tarmac of the Mall. Ball then managed to open the rear car door where Princess Anne was sitting. He grabbed her left arm

116

while Mark Phillips grabbed the right and a "tug-of-war" ensued. "He said I had to go with him," Princess Anne recalled, "and I said I didn't want to. I was scrupulously polite because I thought it would be silly to be too rude at that stage." However, she and Mark Phillips won the tug-of-war and managed to close the door. The sleeve of Princess Anne's blue velvet dress was torn off in the struggle.

What was extraordinary was that there were many passers-by yet nobody went to call for the police. A taxi went past, but the fare insisted that the driver should not stop—the passenger was dropped at Charing Cross Station and the driver returned and the nightmare scene was still happening. In the meantime, Rowena Brassey had been told to go and was crouching by the back wheel of the car. Again it was Princess Anne who recalled that:

She [Rowena Brassey] was going to pick up the policeman's gun but some bossy lady standing on the side of the road told her *not to touch it* in fierce tones. The policeman got back in and joined the fray and got shot again for his pains.

Inspector Beaton had, in fact, put his hand in front of the muzzle of the kidnapper's .22 revolver to shield Princess Anne. He still refused to give up, telling Mark Phillips to release the door so that, although twice wounded, he could kick it open. He tried and failed and was shot for the third time. He rolled out of the car and lay on the pavement with a bullet in his stomach. Meanwhile, Callendar, the chauffeur, had been sitting in his seat with the engine running. Ignoring the gunman's instructions, he tried to get out of the car only to be shot at point blank range. Rowena Brassey said afterwards that the guns did not sound like those on television or the cinema and when the chauffeur was shot, he did not realise it for a few moments, then in a surprised tone said, "Good God, I've been shot!"

All this time, Princess Anne was calmly having a fairly low-key discussion about the fact that she wasn't going to go anywhere and wouldn't it be much better if he'd go away and she would forget all about it, "which was wishful thinking," she said afterwards:

> There were occasional bursts of activity from elsewhere . . . a policeman wandered over and literally tapped the man on the shoulder because I don't think he realised that it was gunshot, and he got shot, wounded, fortunately not seriously.

That policeman was PC Michael Hills who was on duty outside St. James's Palace: the official version was that he fully grasped the situation, grabbed the man by the elbow and was shot in the stomach. It was he that finally summoned the police on his radio. Another of the "bursts of activity" was the arrival of Brian McConnell, a journalist who had been behind the Royal car in a taxi. Bravely, he approached the gunman saying, "Look, old man, these are friends of mine. Give me the gun". He, too, was shot in the chest. Two more civilians finally came to their rescue, a chauffeur, Glenmore Martin and Ronald Russel. While Martin attended the injured Constable Hills, Mr. Russel punched the gunman twice, who fired at him and missed.

In the car Princess Anne and Mark Phillips were lying on the floor "in a heap". She managed

> to reach the door handle behind my head, and I opened the door and literally did a backward somersault on to the road and then waited because I thought that if I was out of the car he might move, and he did eventually, and went to the front of the car. I got back into the car and shut the door.

Meanwhile, the police had arrived, dozens of them with wailing sirens and angry blue, flashing lights. Mark Phillips realised that this could cause even more danger:

> That was the most frightening moment. I really thought that was it. Up until then, he'd been waving the gun about and threatening us,

but while we'd been talking and arguing we'd managed to keep things on a reasonable level. But then, suddenly we were surrounded by police cars . . . and it was a bit like cornering an animal—there was no escape for him and at that moment I really thought we might have been shot.

Princess Anne, however, was totally in command of the situation, saying to the police, "Go on, there's your chance", and one of them ran along towards St. James's Park and brought him down with a flying tackle. The man who arrested the gunman with that flying rugby tackle was Peter Edwards from the CID. As the gunman was led away, Princess Anne, Mark Phillips and Rowena Brassey went on to the Palace, and the injured were rushed to various London hospitals for emergency operations.

Even after such an ordeal, Princess Anne's first thoughts were for others. She telephoned her parents who were on a Royal Tour to Indonesia, and told the Duke of Edinburgh that, although badly shaken, they were "delighted to be in one piece". Then she spoke to her brother, the Prince of Wales, in San Diego, California on his ship, HMS *Jupiter*. He was all for flying home immediately, but she assured him that there was no need. A very nice touch was to telephone Alison Oliver to put her mind at ease as she knew that she would be worried. Likewise, Mark Phillips telephoned his parents, and also Princess Anne's old schoolfriend with whom they were supposed to be dining.

"Oh", said their hostess, "have you been held up?"

"Well, you could say that," quipped Mark Phillips.

After a full statement to the police, and a restorative glass of whisky for Mark Phillips, they both drove their own cars back to Sandhurst, heavily escorted.

Throughout the whole affair, Princess Anne remained calm, clearheaded and composed. That she had considered such an attack, even assassination, a distinct possibility, did nothing to detract from her undoubted courage and extreme bravery. She recognises "that public figures have always been in danger to some degree". Throughout history, most members of the Royal Family have experienced some form of attack. There were five assassination attempts on Queen Victoria alone; her son, Edward VII, when Prince of Wales narrowly missed the assassin's bullet in Belgium (he kept the bullet). During the Second World War, a deranged soldier found his way into the Queen's (Queen Elizabeth the Queen Mother) bedroom. More recently, an intruder entered the Queen's bedroom and sat on the end of her bed, blood dripping from his hand. During the start of the 1981 Trooping the Colour, a man in the crowded Mall managed to fire off six rounds, fortunately all blanks, at the Queen as she rode past.

Apart from the murder of Earl Mountbatten of Burma (and two of his family and a friend) by the IRA, these attacks have been made by single people. Princess Anne believes that the "greatest danger is the lone nutcase who has just got enough to put it together rather than the organised terrorist group". (The IRA immediately disclaimed any part of that kidnap attempt.) Today, the Royal Family, with their increased number of public engagements and their "walkabouts", are much at risk. In a chilling indictment of the times, Princess Anne admitted that "it would be fair to say that if anyone was seriously intent on wiping one out, it would be very easy to do."

Although Mark Phillips as a serving officer had sworn to defend Queen and country, his part in the affair should not be underrated. Not believing that such a thing could ever happen, unlike Princess Anne, he had not made any "contingency plans". Throughout the attack, he did try to shield her with his body, not always easy in a car. Later, he was to admit unashamedly that he was very frightened. He did, however, keep his head and, as his wife pointed out jokingly, kept "out of the way of the bullets". With the number of bullets and amount of shattered glass that was flying around, it is amazing that neither of them was hurt. He did not feel that he had done "anything particularly brave—but I didn't do anything stupid either which might have made things worse."

Before leaving for Oak Grove, Princess Anne issued a statement:

We are very thankful to be in one piece. But we are deeply disturbed and concerned about those who got injured, including our chauffeur Mr. Callendar and Inspector Beaton. Inspector Beaton acted particularly bravely and, although shot, he continued to protect us. We are extremely grateful to all those members of the police and public who tried to help us.

Inside Buckingham Palace everything was calm and well ordered, in fact the whole thing, according to the BBC's Court Correspondent, "was rather like the American notion of how the British behave in a crisis . . . *Mrs. Miniver, The Bridge over the River Kwai*, cups of tea in the blitz, that kind of atmosphere". The Press Association's correspondent, Douglas Dumbrell, was there too within minutes of their arrival at the Palace—the Press Association had been tipped off by their Northern Ireland office as the mother of one of their reporters had witnessed the scene and alerted her son in Belfast. Miss Anne Hawkins (now Mrs. Michael Wall) was the Press Secretary on duty that night who managed everything with "a dignified calm". As the corre-

123

spondents waited in an ante-room, a woman's voice gave a clear account of what had happened that night over the Palace loud-speaker system. Only later, did they discover that it was Rowena Brassey speaking from first-hand experience of the "Mall Incident".

Later, the whole bizarre story of the kidnap attempt came out. Ian Ball was just such a man as Princess Anne described as the most dangerous—"the lone nut-case who has got just enough to put it together". Aged twenty-six and a petty criminal, he had a serious record of psychiatric illness. A total nonentity, he was not unlike the baker in ancient Rome who murdered a patrician in the Senate. When asked why he did it, he replied that no one would ever remember a mere baker—but the murderer of a patrician goes down in history. However, Ball was not only looking for fame but money too. He was frighteningly well organised. A ransom note was found on him addressed to the Queen. In it, he demanded £3 million to be paid in five-pound notes, all "used, unmarked, not sprayed with any chemical substance and not consecutively numbered". He had clearly thought that he would have to kill a policeman as he demanded a free pardon for that, the kidnap, even any violation of the Exchange Control Act in perpetuity. The Queen was to go to see him and give a sample signature "to prove that she really was the Queen". He was also to remain anonymous and, if the law would not permit it, then the law was to be changed. Also, a private plane was to be put at his disposal to fly him to Zurich. He had everything worked out to the last detail. He had watched her movements, rented a house to keep her in during the negotiations and destroyed everything that could identify him— including his amateur pilot's licence. Two months later he came up before Lord Chief Justice Widgery at the Old Bailey and pleaded guilty to the attempted kidnap and the attempted murder of two police officers and two civilians. He was described as mad "by any standard" and "potentially suicidal and homicidal and in need of treatment." His only defence was that he wanted to "draw attention to the lack of facilities for treating mental illness under the National Health Service". He was sentenced to be detained "without limit of time" at a special hospital prison.

While the police and government were busy ordering all kinds of inquiries, those who were wounded were recovering in hospital. Both Princess Anne and Mark Phillips visited them and thanked them for their part in the affair. Inspector Beaton received the highest peace-time award, the George Cross, the George Medal going to Constable Hill and Roland Russel. The Queen's Gallantry Medal was awarded to Brian McConnell, Detective Inspector Edwards who made the actual arrest and Mr. Callendar, the chauffeur. At the investiture, the Queen was able to thank them personally for saving her daughter and son-in-law's lives, but pointed out that it was purely their gallantry that was being rewarded regardless of whom they saved. On the Princess's birthday, the Queen created her a Dame Grand Cross of the Royal Victorian Order for her "calm and brave behaviour", and "the Queen also wishes to recognise the excellent conduct of Captain Mark Phillips and Miss Rowena Brassey." He was made a Commander of the Royal Victorian Order and Miss Brassey became a member of the Order, fourth class. Awards of the Royal Victorian Order are made personally by the monarch and are generally given for services to the sovereign and her family.

The major result of the kidnap attempt was that security round all members of the Royal Family was stepped up. Oak Grove basked in its floodlights at night and Army patrols kept a twenty-four hour surveillance on the house. Today, all cars used by members of the Royal Family have been specially modified with automatic locking devices, bullet-proof glass and radio equipment. Back-up cars with plain clothes officers are also in constant radio communication wherever they go.

Princess Anne laments, but appreciates, the necessity of such security today. Nor is it up to them to decide what level of security they wish as if anything were to go wrong, then it would be the police and the government that would be responsible. Princess Anne has said that before the kidnap attempt, security

was much more low-key, but there is a combination of things that have happened since then which has made it much more difficult, and I think that all of us have to accept that it is a problem, but when we are at home I think, within our own sphere, then of course we can be that much freer. Obviously it is much more difficult I think for people, perhaps the more senior members of the family, who didn't have such a high level of security, that it has become more so, but for the younger members it's been around more obviously all their lives. It's perhaps easier to become accustomed to. Having said that, it would be nice every now and again, not to have it at all.

Although Princess Anne says that the greatest threat to her security are loners, acting on their own, the threat of large-scale operations moving in is always there. During her latest visit to Brazil to see a gala performance of the Sadlers Wells Ballet in March 1986, a plot to kidnap her was discovered by the Brazilian police. It was suspected that supporters of Juan Carlos de Reis, a notorious cocaine smuggler, were planning to abduct her and hold her hostage for their leader —de Reis, known as Eschadina, Portuguese for

Little Ladder, had already escaped three times from prison. Security by the Brazilian police was tightened around Princess Anne and, according to the Embassy bulletin, "they took all necessary precautions". Part of these precautions was to use the Ambassador's wife, Mrs. John Ure, to take Princess Anne's place in the Royal car. Princess Anne carried on as if nothing had happened and returned, seemingly unconcerned, just in time to compete in the Brigstock Horse Trials.

The men who guard the members of the Royal Family are all volunteers from the Royal Protection Squad. They are on duty every hour of every day, and always accompany their charges whenever they leave home. They become very much part of the team, after all, they see more of their employer than they do of their own family (Princess Anne's detective has a room at her home, Gatcombe Park). Often, they become more like an equerry than a bodyguard—it was not unusual to see photographs of Princess Anne at a horse trials with her detective carrying her saddle or minding one of her children.

Living and working in such close proximity can have its problems. In 1985 it was alleged that Sergeant Peter Cross, Princess Anne's detective, was returning to uniformed duties from the Royal Protection Squad for being "over-familiar" with his employer. A common kindness of Princess Anne is to invite former staff down to Gatcombe for a day out in the country, and to see their old friends. When Cross was asked, he obviously misread the gesture. When he left the police force, he offered the account of "his friendship" with Princess Anne to Fleet Street for a reputed £200,000. Eventually, the *News of the World* serialised the story over two Sundays. It produced a furore. The public were generally outraged: Geoffrey Dickens, Conservative MP for Littleborough, called for an amendment to the overworked Official Secrets Act to "stamp out this despicable, sneaky practice" while his former wife let out that "he's a very convincing liar. I don't know what to believe". Princess Anne merely laughed it off as she does with all such stories.

However close the security, there is always the threat of danger. Even now, Mark Phillips admits that he is still slightly nervous in traffic or a crowd if someone does something unusual or unexpected. Princess Anne and her detectives are ever wary too. When she attended a large dinner-party at Maxim's, the restaurant off Leicester Square, in November 1984, there was a sudden burst of "machine-gun fire" from outside. Her detectives rushed over to the table, forcing her to the floor. The other guests, who included Michael Palin, Denholm Elliott, Anthony Andrews and Maggie Smith, sat stunned, until it was announced that it was just a firework display put on to mark the opening of a nightclub nearby.

One particularly unpleasant event for Princess Anne occured back in 1975 when she received a series of anonymous telephone calls at Oak Grove. The man repeatedly called on her private telephone number but never long enough for him to be traced. The calls were either obscene or just a nuisance: "Hello Anne . . . it's me. I know you but you don't know me" or else he whistled the National Anthem. At other times, they were of the "heavy breathing" variety. The telephone was then tapped in a bid to catch the caller but without success. When her private number was changed and the calls persisted, it narrowed the field down to "an inside job", and not long after an embarrased spokesman from the Post Office declared that "after pretty intensive investigations into the matter a member of our staff has resigned".

And so, at the end of the first two years of her marriage, Princess Anne had carved out several names for herself. She had become the Three-Day Event European Champion at the age of twenty-one. She had provided a spectacle at her wedding to lift the nation from gloom. But it was her bravery, courage and supreme self-control during the kidnap attempt that really showed what she was made of. She had set the pattern of her life.

7

At Home at Gatcombe Park

WITH characteristic independence, Princess Anne has always lived her life at a pace dictated by her alone. Apart from her official duties, she refuses to pander to public demand or taste. Her views are definite, her replies carefully considered. When asked by Marjorie Proops in 1976 when she was going to have a baby (as opposed to being told every other week by the foreign press that she was pregnant), she thought that:

> having a family can wait a bit longer. I know that some people think that you should have your children sooner rather than later, when you are closer to them in age, but I am not so sure. My own family is a splendid example of inconsistency. There was one lot when my mother was very young and a second lot later on. But I don't think you are settled enough at the beginning of your marriage to have children.

It was not until they had bought their present house and estate that their future looked less transitory. They could really settle down then and start a family.

Mark Phillips's two-year attachment to the Royal Military College came to an end in March 1976. His regiment was then serving in Northern Ireland. It was even more unthinkable that he should rejoin them there, as it was for Princess Anne to have gone to Germany after they married. Instead, he was posted to the Ministry of Defence in Whitehall: GSO 3 in Army Training. Although no longer instructing at Sandhurst, he was, of course, still in the Army and therefore entitled to a quarter. Princess Anne had spent a large sum of money on Oak Grove, so at least they could reap some further benefit from her investment if they stayed there for a while. To move to London was impracticable; too far from the horses and nowhere suitable to live—all that was on offer was either her three-roomed apartment in Buckingham Palace or Kensington Palace, which in any case, was either full or uninhabitable. So they began looking for a home in the country.

There was no great rush to find a house so long as Mark Phillips stayed in the Army. As both Princess Anne and he were working in London, they thought that they should be within striking distance of the capital. Unfortunately, everyone else who had rusticated and still worked in London had the same idea. Their searches took them to the Home Counties, within a radius of sixty miles of London; they looked particularly around Windsor and made a tour of the available Grace and Favour houses. It was confirmed by the Crown Commissioners that they were about to take Forest Lodge, a fine fourteen-bedroomed Georgian house within Windsor Great Park, but Buckingham Palace denied the rumour. Buckingham Palace was correct.

Where Princess Anne has always said that she would prefer a small, manageable home, she in fact needs a substantial house. Although they had no children at that time, they were certainly planned, and that meant day and night nurseries and room for a nanny. There had to be a room for a lady-in-waiting for those early starts or late engagements, and a room for the detective. Then more spare rooms and bathrooms for guests. Anne needs a dresser, a cook and a butler. She also has to have formal rooms for entertaining, and a study each for her and Mark Phillips. With the restrictions placed upon him, Mark Phillips realised that he could not stay in the Army for ever, and that once he left he would have to find some form of gainful employment. Apart from soldiering, all he knew about was riding and training event horses. Both he and Princess Anne had built up a fine string of horses with "followers", so the house they bought had to have enough land to accommodate their ever-growing stable.

At that time, nothing was suitable in the area they had chosen. They looked further afield, to Wiltshire (the Phillips parents' county) and Gloucestershire. One house they considered quite seriously was Copse Hill House, near Stow-on-the-Wold in the Cotswolds, the former home of Major David Fleming, nephew of the creator of James Bond. Another was Highgrove, near Tetbury, the present home of the Prince and Princess of Wales. Each house had some major drawback, in the case of Highgrove it was too large and too near the road. Often, it was the price that put them off; as soon as the vendor's agents heard who the purchaser was, the price crept up.

It is likely that the Queen offered to buy her daughter and son-in-law a small estate, for, had they found a place to their liking, they would not have been able to pay for it. At that time, Mark Phillips was drawing a salary from the Army of around £4,500 and possibly an allowance from his parents. The Phillipses were adequately well off (Major Phillips farmed three hundred acres, was a director of Walls, the ice-cream and sausage manufacturers, and had an interest in a quarry that sold out at the top of the market) but not rich enough to finance his son in buying a large agricultural estate. On her marriage, Princess Anne's grant from the Civil List was increased from £15,000 to £35,000 a year, but, with her increased outgoings and costs, and even the most careful of house-keeping, she could not have managed it on her own. They could afford the running of a large house, but the buying of it would be outside their pockets.

Their patience was finally rewarded when the Conservative elder statesman, Lord (Rab) Butler of Saffron Waldon, the Master of Trinity College, Cambridge, heard that they were looking for a house in Gloucestershire and wrote offering them his estate, Gatcombe Park with its 733 acres. The house was built about 1770 by Edward Sheppard on the proceeds from his success in producing a vastly improved fleece from crossing his Ryeland sheep with the newly introduced Spanish Merino. His son sold the house and estate to David Ricardo, the son of a Dutch Jew who had made a fortune dealing on the London Stock Exchange. He retired to Gatcombe to study the classical theory of political economy and later entered the House of Commons. He commissioned George Basevi, a gifted pupil of Sir John Soane and kinsman of Disraeli, to remodel the house in the 1820s. Since then, the place had remained largely unaltered.

The exterior is typical of the second half of the eighteenth century. It is a handsome grey house with two storeys and a basement, and a finely moulded cornice and balustraded parapet. The front is made more interesting with an open pediment above a Venetian window opening onto a balcony above the porch, which has four Doric columns. On either side are one-storied wings in the same style as the central block. It appears larger than it really is by the addition of a conservatory built on to the west front in 1829.

A great-grandson of David Ricardo sold the estate in 1940 to Samuel Courtauld who in turn, left it to his son-in-law, another politician, R. A. Butler. By the time Princess Anne and Mark Phillips went to see it, it had not been lived in as a whole house for at least ten years. Before that it had been let to a series of tenants. When Princess Anne and Mark Phillips drove down the pot-holed drive with banks of scrubby laurel sweeping the car, past a dilapidated coach house, and arrived at the crumbling Georgian house, they were both excited at what they had found. The house had instant appeal. Mark Phillips later recalled: "We stood on the front steps and looked out at the view; it was quiet, it was secluded, it was peaceful with woods down each side of a long valley. I thought to myself—well, whatever is inside we can change, given time. But this we can never change. This is just what we have been looking for." The "we" was not the Royal "we".

Inside, they were met with a scene of largely total dilapidation. The walls were damp and grimy; the plumbing antedeluvian and the wiring in the same parlous state. The kitchen was large, damp and dirty with an old coal-burning range and an antiquated water-tank. With the vogue for bathrooms after the turn of the century, the first floor had been unimaginatively converted with the bathrooms at the front of the house with the best view and the bedrooms behind overlooking tumble-down sheds. That being said, the superb quality of the interior, as described below by Sir Nicholas Pevsner, was unmistakable.

The entrance hall gives on to the main staircase, which is partly screened from it by a pair of tall Doric columns. The east side contains the dining room. The library is beyond in a single-storied wing, with bookcases evidently designed by Basevi. Behind this is a kitchen with a domed roof. The west side has two drawing-rooms and the conservatory beyond. The principal rooms have carved marble chimney-pieces; one in a bedroom is made of onyx, with ormalu decoration. Good stone vases in the grounds, which are splendidly landscaped. The stables are built round a polygonal yard with an embattled wall facing the buildings.

However, they realised that however costly the repair and renovation would be, in the end, they would have the perfect home. Lord Butler's agents who handled the sale enthused about the house in typically rosy-hued terms: "It is a super property. It really is a wonderful place and just perfect for people who want seclusion. Obviously, young people moving into a house want to make certain changes but they could move straight in if they wanted." The Phillipses returned several times, bringing the Queen and Prince Philip over from Badminton after the horse trials in April.

Finally, the details were worked out between the Queen and Lord Butler and the completion date set for Michaelmas, 29 September 1976. Lord Butler, who thought "the deal was really clinched by the Queen" because she liked the place so much, added that he was "delighted that the Princess and her husband had decided to buy it. I really wouldn't have wanted to part with it to anyone else." The press made much of the purchase, speculating that the Queen paid a sum "in the region of £750,000". The sale price was in fact nowhere near that figure. The house needed a great deal of money spending on it, the land—five hundred acres of arable and 250 acres of woodland—needed "a Herculean task of reclaiming and taming a formidable acreage of recalcitrant land . . . Gatcombe had just been ticking over for some years." Erring on the purchaser's side, a sum of £500,000 would have been a good price.

Inevitably, censure came from the left wing of the Labour Party. A motion was tabled that the "provision of fifty houses for families in need

would have been a much more worthy investment in these days of public spending cuts".
Labour MPs called this "flaunting of wealth
appalling and almost obscene", while Denis
Skinner pointed out that: "Last year the
Commons was told the Royal Family was
bordering on the point of bankruptcy. Hundreds
of MPs were lured into the voting lobby to
increase their substantial holdings. Now the
truth is out." While being good anti-monarchist
material, Mr. Skinner's statement was far from
accurate. The Queen paid for Gatcombe out of
her own monies which had nothing to do with
the Civil List, the grant voted annually to her
from the Government. One newspaper source
came up with the fact that there were eighty-two
rooms in the "mansion"—in fact, counting every
room and extra-large cupboards, there are,
according to Mark Phillips, only thirty-two.

While the farming operation continued to tick
over under the farm manager, Princess Anne and
Mark Phillips approached the enormous job of
renovating the house. The bedrooms were to be
put back to the front of the house and a self-
contained nursery flat made out of the rabbit-
warren of maids' rooms on the top floor. The
kitchen and pantry were redesigned to bring
them up to the twentieth century. Before
anything else, the house had to be rewired and
replumbed and a modern central-heating system
installed. Then there was the wet rot and the dry

rot to eradicate. An elaborate burglar alarm and security system was also required. As Oak Grove was still their principal residence, there was no question of using any of Princess Anne's grant from the Civil List on renovating Gatcombe. Instead, they pooled their capital and made up the difference with a mortgage.

The builders arrived in January 1977 amid much local excitement, and the inevitable criticism when it was seen that they were employing a London firm as opposed to local labour. They worked on the house throughout the spring and summer. Having an interior designer within the family, Princess Anne went to David Hicks (he married Lord Mountbatten's younger daughter, Pamela). Hicks, who specialises in houses of that period, drew up an elaborate plan for the decor. In the end, it turned out to be too expensive to follow completely, and only certain aspects were retained—the traditional Georgian colours of pale apricot for the hall, soft apple-green and cream for the drawing-room and Princess Anne's sitting-room beyond, a rich, red dining room and russet for Mark Phillips's study.

Although the house would be all that they ever needed, there were no proper stables. The existing stables, built round the polygonal yard, were dilapidated and too old-fashioned and impractical to restore. Five years later, planning permission was granted to turn the old stable-block into accommodation for students of the

Royal Agricultural College, Cirencester. Instead, they decided to build a new stable-block with fifteen loose-boxes, designed by Mark Phillips based on those he had seen abroad. After careful costing, the price was held down to £35,000. As the mortgage money and their capital was being swallowed up by the house, the money to pay for the stables was raised by the sale of two promising novice-event horses and the insurance money received from the death of Doublet. Again, the carpers had a field day. A price of £100,000 was put on the building works, the old chestnut of using Civil List money was revived, or that they were using their mortage money. Mark Phillips was requoted, out of context, saying that "we are just like any other couple with a mortgage" inferring that his horse venture was depriving *everyone* in the country who could not raise a mortgage for a home. Worse, it was added that there was a swimming pool for the horses. They ignored these jibes at the time, but three years later in her interview for *The Observer* Princess Anne used the claim to illustrate how "stories go round":

When we built the stables . . . one box was made the same size as the others, but with the floor two feet lower. This means that you can fill the box with water up to eighteen inches. When horses have got sore feet or bruises to their lower legs, the ancient remedy is to apply hot, then cold, then hot water. Normally you'd use a hose, but if you can put the water into the box, it makes life much easier. Somebody wrote a newspaper story saying that we built a swimming pool for the horses.

In the late summer, Mark Phillips approached his neighbour, Captain Vaisey Davis, with the thought of buying a couple of fields that "went" better with Gatcombe than with Aston Farm. Instead of negotiating for the small parcel of land, he was to his great surprise offered the whole farm of 533 acres. It put him in a turmoil. It obviously made sound economic farming sense to run the two farms together but neither he nor Princess Anne had anything to buy it with. He approached several institutions, pension-fund managers and insurance companies with a view to a lease-back arrangement whereby the company owned the land and the Phillipses became tenants. It was a widely practised arrangement then when farming land was a good investment. Negotiations were going well and they detailed their plans to the Queen over dinner one night. According to Mark Phillips, she replied, "Why can't I be the institution—why can't I buy it, and rent it to you in the same way?" In October, the Queen became the owner of Aston Farm, her daughter and son-in-law, the tenants. By this stroke of good fortune they had a viable estate, though they had a long way to go yet. Their new acquisition was tactfully described by George Whitlock, author of *Royal Farmers* as having been once farmed "quite progressively, [but] bore the evidence of having been the property of a man over ninety years old".

"We did the thing you should never do," Princess Anne admitted, "have a baby and move house at the same time." Princess Anne celebrated their fourth wedding anniversary, 14 November 1977, with a small family dinner at Buckingham Palace. In the early hours of the next morning, she woke her husband who took her to the Lindo Wing of St. Mary's Hospital, Paddington. The precedent for Royal births there was set by the Duchess of Gloucester, who had her first child, the Earl of Ulster, there prematurely by caesarean section. St. Mary's was chosen simply because the Queen's gynaecologist, Mr. George Pinker, who also attends the other female members of the Royal Family, is one of the hospital's consultant obstetricians and gynaecologists. At 10.46 a.m., Princess Anne's baby was born, a healthy 7lb 9oz boy. The father, who was present throughout the labour and the birth, telephoned the news to the Queen. The Queen was about to hold an investiture in the Throne Room when she made her own announcement ten minutes later: "I apologise for being late, but I have just had a message from the hospital. My daughter has given birth to a son, and I am now a grandmother." She was patently thrilled at the birth of her first grandchild, and those waiting in the Throne Room shared her delight with an involuntary cheer. It was to be a double celebration as the Duchess of Gloucester gave birth to her second child, a daughter, two days after Princess Anne.

A few days later Princess Anne and her unnamed son left hospital. The public were generally pleased with the news of the birth. They had warmed to Mark Phillips and his initial remark to reporters on the birth of his son: "Well, it's nice to think I've done something right for a change", was an obvious reference to criticisms of his supposed extravagance at Gatcombe. Predictably, Willie Hamilton declared, "How charming—another one for the payroll." Auberon Waugh, reworking the Queen's remark about the possibility of her four-legged grandchildren, wrote in his *Private Eye* diary column that he thought:

Princess Anne, Dame Anne Phillips has given birth to a centaur. So it is hard to decide whether one should congratulate her on her good fortune or commiserate with her. It happens in the best families. The best thing is surely to enter him for Eton and for Fred Winter's stable at Lambourn and decide which is more suitable nearer the time.

The safety lobby even took a swipe at Princess Anne as she sat in the front seat of the car with her baby: it was an "appalling" example to mothers. Since seat-belts have become compulsory, it is now illegal to have a baby in the front of the car. Ten days after the birth, Mark Phillips drove his wife and son, Peter, down to their new home, Gatcombe Park, to begin the next phase of their lives.

When asked if it were harder for her to keep her privacy today than when she was a child, Princess Anne replied that she thought that it was the ratio of public to private life for members of the Royal Family that had changed:

If you look back on the Royal Family in the past, if anything they had *less* public life, but more of their private life "showed" . . . They had much larger households, a much more spectacular daily life—as the aristocracy did in those days—everything about them was big news in the newspapers.

If the King and Queen went from the house of one friend to another, it was news. Not today. It seems to me that the Royal Family is more in the public eye because of the number of *public* functions it is involved in. And because its private life is much less spectacular I don't think there is the same degree of interest in it. Interest in us [the Royal Family] is polarised if you like. But I think it would be six of one and half-a-dozen of the other.

Of course, the more people want to know about you, the more you are going to polarise it, the more you're going to separate your public life from your private life. That's not royal, that's human; I think most people would react like that. The more you appear in public, the more there is published about you, the more you want—and need—a real honest-to-goodness *home* life, in proper privacy.

Those two main demands, that of being a royal princess with a busy public life and being a wife and mother could cause a conflict of interests. However, with her thoroughly sensible approach to life, and a generous dish of good fortune, Princess Anne has managed to find the right balance between the two. Her solution to the dual role is quite straightforward: she simply gives her best to the one which most demands her attention. Her home is where her position and her public role do not count. She works hard to keep it so. "You have to have something to call your own," she said to Angela Rippon. "After I've been in public for some days, I *want* to be on my own. A lot of people talk to you, and you talk to a lot of people. It's nice to go off and not talk and be on your own; you *need* it." No wonder she goes for long walks on her own.

Contrary to popular belief, she spends most of her time at Gatcombe. Whereas it would be presumptuous to speculate, and probably inaccurate, that the purchase of Gatcombe and the farmland was the making of their marriage, it certainly provided the answer to the majority of the problems in those early years. It enabled Mark Phillips to resign his commission in the Army and, thanks to the Queen's generosity, become a working farmer. His Army career ended after ten years in April 1978. He was sorry to leave. Princess Anne shared in his disappointment, as she thought that

it was a pity, but it was more or less forced on him. If he had been able to do what he wanted to, which was basically stay to command a squadron and then possibly the regiment, I would have been very happy, though I don't suppose that I would have made a very good colonel's wife. . . . But he was never going to be in a position to do that, and there wouldn't have been much point in his spending the rest of his life behind a desk in Whitehall.

To further his new profession, Mark Phillips enrolled on the intensive farming course at the Royal Agricultural College, Cirencester. The farm could be made to provide an income, and their horses could be kept and, to a degree, fed.

A countryman born and bred, he is in his element at Gatcombe. He never wanted, nor was indeed able, to run in the "Royal Stakes", and consequently never shone when asked to compete, although Princess Anne thinks that now he "copes very well". She is perfectly content for him to remain at home, doing what he is best at:

He's remarkable really, in a sense that it [attending engagements] really doesn't bother him. He comes on some trips abroad. But I'm sure it's right that he's in a position to have his own life and doesn't have to come on many more trips, because I think he'd hate that.

Gatcombe has also given Mark Phillips another dimension to his life. A great deal of hard work has gone into improving the house and the estate. He is contented there and proud of his achievements; he has made something to hand down to his children. He is the undoubted boss at home, genuinely earning the respect of the estate staff and grooms, and his wife once admitted that he could be "very stubborn". In her marriage vows, Princess Anne promised to "obey" her husband. It is, of course, easier for a wife to respect a man who is building a life, is masterly in his home and successful in his chosen pastime, rather than a man fumbling around in the wrong job, making an ass of himself. Those

148

who call him "Fog" (wet and thick) and see him
blundering on a television chat show should
listen to him instructing his riding pupils before
forming an opinion of him. At home, his former
nickname of "Chief" is more appropriate.

Princess Anne is also extremely happy with
her lot as a farming partner. When asked if she
had been born a boy, would she have liked to
have joined the Royal Navy, she replied:

Farming, the country life, goes very much
with the family. To a great extent, I have been
brought up in it. I think if I'd been asked that
question before I was married I would have
said, "Farming is the way I would like to live
more than any other, because that's the way I
grew up, and now that we are farming, I find
it fun to be involved in it more closely.

"Being pregnant is an occupational hazard of
being a wife," Princess Anne remarked shortly
before the birth of their second child, a
daughter, in May 1981. Within four days, she
was back at Gatcombe. There was great speculation for three weeks as to what the girl would
be called, but no one, not even Auberon Waugh
of *Private Eye*, predicted the final choice of
Zara. Zara, a Greek biblical name which trans-
lates as "bright as the dawn", was suggested by
Prince Charles. Her parents liked the name, a
complete departure from anything Royal.

Auberon Waugh did not, as he revealed in his *Diary*:

> So it is to be Zara. The reason for this strange name I learn is that the happy couple intended to call their darling little occupational hazard "Sarah", but the rest of the world misunderstood their strange pronunciation.
>
> So now the poor little thing is stuck with a Jewish boys' name from the Book of Chronicles for the rest of her life. If ever I meet the unfortunate child, I shall call her Susan.

Although their mother is a princess and styled Her Royal Highness, both Peter and Zara Phillips are, like their father, commoners. Contrary to popular belief, Mark Phillips was not offered a title as in the case of Lord Snowdon when he married Princess Margaret so there was no question of him turning the honour down. Thus, his children are plain Master and Miss, even though they are seventh and eighth respectively in line to the throne.

Like most of the "old guard" nannies, the Royal ones are used to moving around within the family and caring for the new generation. The faithful "Alla" (Clara Knight) who was nanny to the later Strathmore children and in particular Lady Elizabeth Bowes Lyon, the present Queen Mother, was recalled from a sister when she in turn needed a nanny for her children. When

Princess Anne needed a nanny for Peter, her former nanny, Mabel Anderson, was available (Prince Edward aged thirteen hardly needed her services). Four years later, in the *Sun*, it was reported that there had been a "blazing row" between Princess Anne and her nanny and that "she had walked out". Whatever the truth of the story, she was replaced by a non-Royal nanny, taking the Phillips children yet one step further outside the Royal sphere of influence. Princess Anne is particularly keen to spare her children the glare of public attention. From her *Observer* interview:

> Again, it's a question of balance. On the one hand you say, "He must be allowed to live a normal life", and you try to keep him out of the limelight as much as possible. On the other hand, he has to know that it is there, otherwise the shock when the limelight comes is going to be awful. I hope that at any rate he'll get through his school career without too much trouble. . . . At the end of the day, people are always going to refer to him as "the grandson of the Queen".

Princess Anne refuses to be drawn on the subject of her children. When asked on Radio 4's *Tuesday Call* what were their likes and dislikes, she gave the standard reply, "I am rather waiting for the children to tell you themselves when they are a bit older. I think at this stage in their careers, the less people know about them the better." While Peter enjoys his father's company around the estate, Princess Anne is particularly indulgent towards her daughter.

Peter Phillips started school on an ordinary level, joining twenty-five other three-year-olds in a playgroup held in the Scout hut in the village. It was a popular move, one local remarking that he was "delightfully surprised when Princess Anne brought her son along. It's very neighbourly." Zara is now at the same school, while Peter went on to the Blueboy School before going to his prep school, Port Regis, at Motcombe Park in Dorset. Princess Anne is still shielding her children from that limelight. Just as she lived by the boards of the pologround as a child, so Peter and Zara spend much of their time at horse trials. Inevitably, they are a source of interest to the public and an obvious subject for photographers. Once, Peter asked why one cameramen was taking photographs of him, when the woman that Princess Anne was with quickly replied, "It's not you they are photographing, but me." Obviously such screening can not last forever.

At home Princess Anne leads the life typical of any wife of a well-off working farmer, a life dominated by horses, dogs, children and the agricultural sequence. Despite the many insights into the lives of the Royal Family, there is still an unbelievable mystique about them. Those who meet Princess Anne for the first time come away with remarks like "she was so natural", as if they were expecting to meet some divine body. The same goes for her home. Those journalists and biographers who visit Gatcombe for the first time are still struck by the informality of the place. That they should use such expressions as the most "unRoyal of Royal households", presupposes they put them down to a life of footmen in knee-breeches and powdered wigs, a butler in a morning coat and wing collar and a series of gilded drawing rooms. Instead, they are surprised to find a comfortable and practical country house, chickens in the drive and copies of *Farmer's Weekly* and *Horse and Hound* on the table. The butler wears jeans and an open-necked shirt, except of course, for formal occasions. Leading such a busy life, there is no time to stand on ceremony; in any case, formality is totally out of the Phillips character. They do not change for dinner, unlike the older generation of the Royal Family, who still put on black tie every night, even if dinner is served on a tray in front of the television.

On non-working days, Princess Anne's routine is little different to any woman with young children living on a farm. In term-time, she drives Zara to school, then the rest of the day is taken up with the horses. "If you are really involved with horses", she has said, "and want to be successful with them . . . not just play at it, they don't leave you much time for anything else." Most of her equestrian time is taken up with her own horses—hours and hours of training or just exercising. Even if she has an engagement in the day, she will always try to fit in one ride before she goes off. Usually, she rides out with her husband, one or two of the grooms and the dogs. Besides Mark Phillips's two gun dogs, there are three dogs, "of varying sizes", that live in at Gatcombe. One is a large black-and-tan foxhound called Random, a present from Sir Rupert Buchanan-Jardine, master of the Dumfriesshire hunt. Random replaced Pleasure, also ex-Dumfriesshire pack, a dog of high intelligence and a sweet nature. After Mark Phillips' parents had taken on the ailing black labrador, Moriarty, the star of the engagement photographs, he was replaced by a lurcher called Laura. Princess Anne explained on *Tuesday Call* that a lurcher is "a sort of poacher's dog. It's a cross between a greyhound and a collie and is very fast, and a thief. We don't trust him in the kitchen." There is also a corgi called Apollo, which is supposed to be looked after by the children, but, like every household, never is. He is a "refugee from my mother's collection of dogs, because he's a dog and she only has bitches". Being a "laid-back" dog, it rarely stirs outside the policies of Gatcombe.

In winter, Princess Anne hunts. Gatcombe is

in the heart of the Beaufort country, and she wears the "blue and buff" (their distinctive coat) of a subscriber. Occasionally, she has a day with another pack, but, unlike Prince Charles who hunts as much as three or four times a week, she rarely has more than one day. She enjoys hunting. It gives her a chance to meet her neighbours, and not least some of her relations—her brother or Prince and Princess Michael of Kent are all subscribers. A day's hunting sometimes helps to sharpen up the younger event horses. As a day's hunting in the middle of winter is usually over by four o'clock, she can make an evening engagement in London. There used to be a vociferous anti-hunting lobby who condemned her in the field and in many column inches in the press, but even they have quietened down. With her new interest in race-riding, she and Mark Phillips often ride out for their neighbour, David Nicholson, as well as schooling his 'chasers and hurdlers over fences.

Working so hard on her horses does not leave Princess Anne with much time to devote to other amusements. However, she still enjoys sailing, although admits to being sea-sick. She also enjoys driving, which is fortunate considering the distance from Gatcombe to her "office", Buckingham Palace, and the miles she drives round the country. When dining in the mess of the Argyll and Sutherland Highlanders, she met a young subaltern, David Stewart of Appin, who

155

drove her back to Balmoral in his Reliant Scimitar. She was so impressed with his car that she has had Scimitars ever since. Her friend, the former world racing champion Jackie Stewart, (no relation to David) recognises her driving skill which he puts down to her prowess as a horse-woman: "Equestrians are good drivers because they have good hands and good 'seat of the pants' reaction."

One feature of Princess Anne's life is that persistent myths grow up out of a chance remark which is later misquoted. On Michael Parkinson's Australian chat show, she was able to lay one ghost, that she would like to be a lorry-driver. What she did say was that, with her HGV licence, she enjoys driving their vast horse-box and *if* she were not a royal princess she might be quite good as a long-distance lorry-driver. She also admitted on the same programme that travelling in the back of a horse-box during her courtship has made her a more considerate driver. Jackie Stewart also admires her competence on the race track. She has had "a couple of days at Silverstone car-racing circuit. I like driving fast on my own. It's very exciting on an empty road, just concen-trating."

Jackie Stewart and his wife Helen are typical of Princess Anne's friends; interesting, loyal and totally without pretension. They fall into well-defined slots—her old eventing friends, Richard

Meade, Lucinda Green, Jane Bullen, Virginia Holgate and Georgina Simpson and her husband Anthony Andrews, the actor. Some of her friends stem from school, such as Victoria Legge-Bourke, one of her first ladies-in-waiting and her sister-in-law Shân, but the majority have dispersed around the country so she rarely sees them. The same is true of the few friends she made in London before she married. Other friends stem from the landed families, the Marquess of Lothian's daughter, Lady Cecil Cameron and her husband, Donald Cameron younger of Locheil, the Balfour twins, Philadelphia and Clemency and of course one of her mother's ladies-in-waiting, Lady Susan Hussey. Naturally, she appointed her own friends as ladies-in-waiting, women like Mary Carew-Pole, the Countess of Lichfield, Caroline Wallace and Rowena Feilden. But the majority of her friends today come from the country around Gatcombe. "We've set up house here", she says, "more by luck than judgement and it happens to be quite close to where Mark grew up. So there is a nucleus of friends from his earlier life." There are some of her friends there too like the Parker-Bowles at Bolehyde Manor, near Chippenham in Wiltshire. Those who are labelled "friends of HRH" in the press are generally distant acquaintances at best, a single meeting more usual. Princess Anne is always pleased to see her real friends. It is easy for them to see when she is at home (close scrutiny of the Court Circular or the list of Royal engagements for the month in *The Times* will tell them that) than it is for her to invite them. Theirs is generally a relationship where they can simply telephone and drop in.

From school Princess Anne has had the same problem of making friends: the more worthwhile people usually hanging back, while the pushier thrust forward. As she told Georgina Howell in the *Sunday Times*, her parents warned her that some people:

> would want to make friends because of who you were. And I think that was fair comment, and it was important to know that. Not that it only applied to us. I think I've been lucky with the friends I've got. I don't reckon I've very many good friends, but that's partly the life one leads—one doesn't stay still for terribly long."

Certainly Princess Anne's greatest friends are her family. She spends much of her time with them being very much part of the "Royal migration". Since the rash of babies and children in the early sixties, the Queen decided that Sandringham was not large enough for the family Christmas house-party, and instead has them all to stay at Windsor. After Christmas, the house-party that invariably includes Princess Anne and her family moves to Sandringham. Easter and Ascot Week, she is again at Windsor. Holidays, in the accepted sense, outside the sanctuary of the Royal Family are difficult for Princess Anne. Timing can be a problem. However, as January and February are slack periods on the farm and the training for the season's eventing has not started seriously, she can sometimes snatch a week's ski-ing. Fortunately, lying on the beach soaking up the sun in some Mediterranean resort is not her idea of an ideal holiday. Instead, she prefers:

a couple of weeks in Scotland and, if the family were there at the time, specially at Balmoral. Because there you can do as much as you like on your own, or you can do things with other people. It suits many of your moods. And it's very beautiful. I don't really mind if it rains . . .

The advantage of going back to Balmoral is that you know where everything is, and you start the holiday from the first minute. It requires no effort at all, which, for me, is what a holiday should be.

As the Queen is especially fond of her first grandson, having them there is wonderful for her too.

Unlike the Prince of Wales, Princess Anne appreciated what she called "the family bit" that much later in life. Like all converts who become passionate about their new faith, she is at her happiest when surrounded by her family. But they provide more than friendship, for her parents and grandmother, are by her own admission, a constant example to her.

The Queen is, of course, both her mother and her sovereign. When Brian Hoey once asked her if it was difficult to maintain a close relationship with a mother who was also the Queen, she replied:

> I think you've got the question the wrong way round. It's much more difficult to remember that she's Queen than a mother. After all, I've known her longer as a mother than as a Queen, if you see what I mean. She has been Queen most of my life but that's not how I think of her—it's the other way around really."

Although Princess Anne is supposed to be "her father's girl", she is extremely close to the Queen. They speak continually on the telephone, especially when she is out of the country on a visit. Of all his children, Princess Anne is supposed to be her father's favourite: "Perhaps I did spoil her at times." In return, she adores him. It must have been a tremendous source of pride when he saw that she had been entered in the marriage register as "Anne *Mountbatten-*

Windsor", the new family name, instead of just Princess Anne, which would have been normal.

Age has tempered the "cats and dogs" fights of their sibling years, and the Prince of Wales and his sister are now very close. It made a good story for the press to invent a constant rivalry between Princess Anne and her sister-in-law, the Princess of Wales. There was Princess Anne in the heat and squalor of a third-world African country receiving little, if any, coverage in the press while all the Princess of Wales had to do was to wear a new dress and she made the front page. Even *Majesty*, one of the magazines for those dedicated Royal fans, had a smiling Princess of Wales on the front cover while the report of that African trip went largely unrecorded. However, the Princess of Wales was able to set the record straight herself, when Sir Alastair Burnett asked her if she had any sense of living in a state of rivalry with Princess Anne, as is said time and time and time again? She replied:

None at all. Princess Anne has been working incredibly hard for the Save the Children Fund and I am her biggest fan, because what she crams into a day I could never achieve. And we've always hit it off very well and I just think she's marvellous. And the story arose obviously as she wasn't chosen perhaps as a godmother for Harry, which had our child been a girl, the possibility was there—but Harry arrived, so we went to a man.

Both Prince Andrew and Prince Edward are especially close to their sister. Before his marriage in July 1986, home to Prince Andrew was Buckingham Palace and Windsor Castle. Gatcombe, with its relaxed air, provided a happy alternative. He enjoys the company of his brother-in-law, both being keen shots and endowed with a similar sense of humour. Prince Edward has always enjoyed the happy position of the youngest member of any family, and equally appreciates his sister and her family. He, too, fits in with the Gatcombe routine, especially at harvest time, and, unlike Prince Andrew, rides out whenever he is staying.

Before Princess Anne's "renaissance", she consistently shared the bottom ratings of the Royalty popularity polls with her aunt, Princess Margaret. The two princesses have much in common. More quick-witted than their elder sister and brother respectively, they were both indulged by their fathers. They have natural charm and wit, (George VI once admitting that Princess Margaret could "charm the pearl out of an oyster") and both are brilliant mimics. Like Princess Margaret, Princess Anne suffered from the same fate of the public not being ready for their brand of a princess—there are the continual references to her not "matching up to the public's idea of a fairy princess". With the break-up of Princess Margaret's marriage, the Royal Family closed ranks, Princess Anne giving her support as one who was also pilloried over the alleged break-up of her own marriage. The admiration of the two Princesses is mutual. Princess Margaret, just twenty years older than her niece, was the most splendid example of sophistication for her niece to follow, while Princess Margaret has said, "Anne's much more positive than I was. She's much tougher too, she's been brought up in a different atmosphere."

Whenever any of the Royal Family speak of their family in public, they are always given their correct title, never just a Christian name, even when they refer to a former monarch—it is always *King* Henry VIII, (even for Shakespeare's play) or *Queen* Elizabeth I; Mark Phillips invariably refers to his wife in public as Princess Anne, even to their closest friends. The one exception is with Queen Elizabeth, the Queen Mother, whom Princess Anne has been known to refer to as just "Grannie". She knows well the bond between her grandmother and the Prince of Wales; "there is rather a special relationship between the eldest grandson and a grandmother, I think, which is not true of grand-daughters," she has said. Not for nothing does the Queen Mother say, "He's a darling", when referring to him, or that she is "hopelessly biased and completely partisan" when writing about her. Princess Anne once admitted that:

> There is no way she couldn't have had an effect on all of us because she's a very remarkable woman. I think everybody knows enough about her over the years to know what an attractive personality she is, and I think they know too how strong she is, what she has had to bear.
>
> Sometimes when I think of her I find it depressing because I can't see any way that I could ever do what she has done. Of course, you can always try.

There are those who would now disagree with her in that as far as "doing what she has done", Princess Anne has achieved just as much in her own special way. Where no one can refuse the Queen Mother anything, few can refuse a request from her grand-daughter either.

There can be few who would begrudge Princess Anne her happy homelife. Gatcombe is her sanctuary, where she can be Mrs. Mark Phillips, the working farmer's wife, rather than Her Royal Highness The Princess Anne. Part of the strength of the Royal Family is that they are a very close and loving family. Princess Anne has truly inherited those values and strengths.

8

The Job

IN the archives at Windsor Castle there is a
notebook written in the precise hand of the
Duke of York, the future George V. Under
the heading of "Monarchy", he writes:

> The crown is no longer an "Estate of the
> Realm" of itself the executive, but the Queen
> [Victoria] nevertheless retains an immense
> unexhausted *influence* which goes some way to
> compensate for the formal *powers* which have
> been lost; this influence can be exercised in
> various ways:
> a. In the *formation* of Ministries; especially in
> choosing between Statesmen who have a claim
> to lead party;
> b. During the *continuance* of Ministries. The
> Crown possesses *first* the right to be consulted,
> *second* the right to encourage and *third* the
> right to warn. And these rights may lead to a
> very important influence on the course of poli-
> tics, especially as under a system of party
> government, the Monarch alone possesses a
> *continuous political experience*.

His official biographer, Sir Harold Nicolson, confirmed that the King's faith in those principles of Monarchy

> . . . was simple, devout even; but selfless. All that he aspired to do was to serve that principle with rectitude; to represent all that was most straightforward in the national character; to give the world an example of personal probity; to advise, to encourage and to warn. To few men has it been granted to fulfil their aspirations with such completeness.

His second son, George VI, followed his prime example in fulfilling that constitutional role.

Today, the Queen, in this age of marked social change, has continued in that same vein, with the same dedication, service and expertise of her father and grandfather. She works immensely hard across the whole spectrum of her constitutional role. Behind the scenes, as successive Prime Ministers will testify, she is well informed making her, increasingly as her reign lengthens, one of the most fully informed people in the world. Publically, she has done more than any of her predecessors to bring the monarchy to the people. She appears tireless in the number and variety of her public appearances, whether they be a State occasion, like the State Opening of Parliament or a factory visit. Wherever she is, whether in person or seen on television, she appears as her people's sovereign, both at home and on a Royal Tour to a Commonwealth country. She is their representative as Head of State, either as hostess to foreign royalty and dignitaries or as ambassadress on overseas tours; the political and economic value of such tours are easily quantifiable. Besides her political and public roles, the Queen bears such titles as *Fidei Defensor*, (the Defender of the Faith). Not only is she the head of the Church of England, she also stands for Christian family life and Christian morals in largely post-Christian times. She is "the Fount of Honour", approving all honours and awarding those of her own for service to Queen or country. Another important function is that she is titular head of the three arms of the Services, the Royal Navy, the Army and the Royal Air Force.

In upholding the Constitution in the public and private ramifications of its role, the Queen must surely be one of the busiest women in the country. Even Willie Hamilton has conceded more than once that she is "truly professional" in her duties. Her former private secretary, Lord Adeane, wrote of her:

Nobody who does not carry such a burden of responsibility is in a position to appreciate the strain it imposes. The Queen is never absolutely free to do as she likes in the way that ordinary men and women are, or to take a complete holiday. Her job is continuous and she cannot, like other hard-worked people, look forward to a period of retirement at the end of her life.

In George VI's remark (now somewhat over-worked as a cliché) "We are not a family, but a firm", he recognised the part members of his family should play within that institution of the Monarchy. As the constitutional role of the British monarchy is understood, rather than defined (Walter Bagehot in *The English Constitution*, published in 1867, has made the best attempt yet to set it down), so the role of the sovereign's close relations is also undefined. It is understood, however, that their role is simply to be supportive of their sovereign in his or her constitutional duty, to the best of their ability.

As in the case of Princess Anne, these members of the Royal Family obviously do not share in the Queen's constitutional right "to be consulted, to encourage, and to warn" on the political front, but they do help share the work-load. They help to "carry the flag", performing hundreds of public duties between them. They all play their parts on State occasions: two of them at a time act as Councillors of State when the Queen is out of the country. Although the Queen remains head of the Forces they act in honorary roles, Colonels-in-Chief of Regiments and their Royal Navy and Royal Air Force equivalents. Just as the Queen's presence undoubtedly adds a certain dignity to an occasion, so the presence of members of her family make even the mundane visit special. Above all, they are all part of the same, caring team. The Prince of Wales is proud to be part of a monarchy whose greatest function he deems "is the human concern which its representatives have for the people, especially in what is becoming an increasingly inhuman era—an age of computers, machines, multi-national organisations". By dint of hard work and more than her share of human concern, Princess Anne is very much part of what Robert Lacy described as "the performing monarchy".

Since her inaugural engagement of presenting those leeks to the Welsh Guards in 1969, Princess Anne has been steadily taking on a greater workload (as, it has to be said, have most of the other members of the Royal Family). There are few perquisites that go with the job, but she travels in style. If she is not driving herself in her own car, there is a chauffeur-driven limousine to take her to an engagement. If the engagement is far away, then, if available, there are the aircraft of the Queen's Flight: three Andovers and two Wessex helicopters. If it happens to be in the vicinity, the Royal Yacht is placed at her disposal for foreign trips. The long holidays that are supposed to go with the job are invariably interrupted by engagements or coincide with an overseas tour.

As the job is to meet people and be seen, she

is constantly on duty, in the public eye. The ever-attendant photographers with their flash-lights are there to capture every facial expression, billowed skirt or misplaced strand of cotton. As with other members of the Royal Family, when Princess Anne officially attends any play or musical performance, it is she that most of the audience has come to see, to note her reaction to that performance, to see if she laughs at any *risqué* passages. Not least, there is the danger attached to the job, as demonstrated with the Mall Incident. Even the Queen received a direct hit from an egg in her 1986 tour to New Zealand the home of the "walk-about". The possibility of real or chance accidents increases with her work-load, although reports of "near misses" in the press are often exaggerated.

The rewards for such work must be measured in job satisfaction rather than in money. Although her allowance from the Civil List of £120,000 would be vast were it just a salary, there are many expenses to be met from it, whit-tling the figure down to a modest remuneration. The greatest single expense, however, is her household and the staff who operate her office.

Whenever Princess Anne undertakes an official engagement, a notice appears in the Court Circular of *The Times* and the *Daily Telegraph* under the heading "Buckingham Palace", where she has her office. The office is in her old school-room. She obviously believes in the maxim "small is beautiful", for the whole of her public life and most of her private life is run by a staff of four—a private secretary, a personal secretary and two general office secretaries. When Princess Anne began her public life, the Queen lent her one of her ladies-in-waiting, Lady Susan Hussey, which was enough for her first few engagements. As her engagements increased, so she needed someone on a more permanent basis. Lady Susan found Mrs. David Hodgson in late 1969 and she has been Princess Anne's personal secretary ever since. Her job is far more than its name implies, for not only does she look after the employer's private life, but is responsible for organising the financial side as well—the office expenses, the running of her official home, Gatcombe, and its staff (not the estate staff or the grooms), and accounts for the allocation of the Civil List. In those early days, the work came in sudden spates. When Princess Anne won the European Championship there were thousands of letters to be answered, over her wedding the staff was temporarily increased to cope with the flood of mail. Today, she is the acknowledged lynch-pin of the operation.

Princess Anne's first choice in ladies-in-waiting was Mary Dawnay, now Mrs. Richard Carew-Pole. According to Princess Anne, they must be:

good at chatting to people and making them feel comfortable, because that helps me really.

It's no good at all if you get somebody turning up in the morning looking like death, and furious and ratty about life and uncommunicative, and when they go out on a trip they're standing in a corner looking glum and bored. That's no help to anyone, least of all the people at the other end, never mind to me. So it is important that they should be capable of being interested and mixing with the people we meet.

Prospective ladies-in-waiting are approached by an intermediary in case they find it difficult to refuse in person. Mary Dawnay was joined by Rowena Brassey, whom Princess Anne met in New Zealand when she was lady-in-waiting to the wife of the Governor-General. Slowly, as the official engagements increased, the numbers built up to seven: Miss Victoria Legge-Bourke and her sister-in-law the Hon. Shân Legge-Bourke, Mrs. Malcolm Innes, the Countess of Lichfield and Mrs. Malcolm Wallace, her former groom and married to her friend Major Wallace. Ladies-in-waiting are unpaid, although they are reimbursed for their expenses. They are uniformly bright and intelligent, and in complete sympathy with "the boss". They all admire her greatly as a person, and for her capacity for hard work. They enjoy her company, particularly her humour in her asides to the remarks of the public that float

24. Happy, despite the pouring rain, Princess Anne on Doublet, with Mark Phillips, Burghley, 1978.

25/26. Princess Anne's children are taken to horse trials up and down the country.

27. Receiving a poem written by Nyash Mvaimvai
(in the wheelchair) at a centre for handicapped
children, Jairos Jiri, Zimbabwe, November 1982.

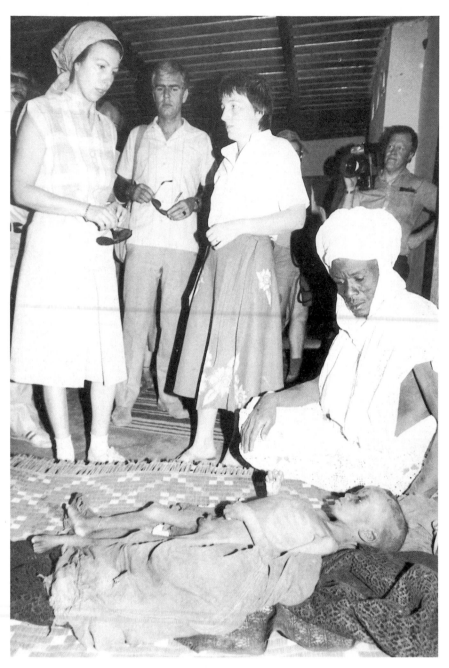

28. The caring Princess in Burkino Fasso (formerly Upper Volta) at a Save the Children Fund Clinic. February 1984.

29. Three popular members of the Royal Family, Princess Anne, the Princess of Wales and Queen Elizabeth the Queen Mother at the première of the film A Passage to India, May 1985.

30. The family team – a trouble shared as Mark Phillips
reflects on the day's placings at the Royal Windsor
Horse Show, May 1985.

31. A long-service badge for one of the ponies at Newton Hall, Swilland, Suffolk, June 1985.

32. Raising money for the disabled, November 1985.

33. Race riding has become a new challenge. Her sixth race riding Little Sloop at Doncaster, March 1986.

34. 150th's celebrations, Paddington Station, April 1986

35. Spattered
with mud,
Cheltenham,
April 1986.

36. At Covent
Garden to mark the
Queen's sixtieth
birthday,
April 1986.

through open car windows during or after an engagement.

Since 1982 the management of Princess Anne's public schedule has been in the care of her private secretary, Lieutenant-Colonel Peter Gibbs. An urbane former Coldstream Guards officer, he has that meticulous eye for detail that is essential for his exacting employer. Joanna Hockley, the secretary, and Petty Officer Wren Susan White complete the team. Being so technically minded, it would not have been surprising if Prince Phillip had been the first to instal a computer in his office, but in fact, it was Princess Anne who recognised its potential.

There is today a certain "breed" of person typical of the various households. Some have even been bred to their position, in-Palace romances and marriages being common. Some members of the households are third and fourth generation. The households are thus a close network of family and friends, cross-referencing throughout the generations and members of the Royal Family. It is much to their employers' credit that members of royal households rarely resign, and when they do, it is generally for some outside reason rather than a clash of personalities. Princess Anne is typical in the way she engenders the loyalty and devoted service of her household.

She has that unique gift of being able to be close to them all, whether salaried or unpaid.

She always uses Christian names, giving them friendship and showing implicit trust in them, but at the same time avoiding becoming familiar. Living in such an informal manner at Gatcombe, she enjoys the same relationship with her staff. When her butler, Mark Simpson, left to work in London as he found the country too lonely, Princess Anne would invite him down for the day or the nanny would bring the children to see him in London. His presence at Gatcombe was greatly missed so he was lured back again with the use of a flat in London for his days off. There is, however, one exception in the length of service with their staff—the fast turnover of cooks, they being like the one described by Saki: "She was good as good cooks go, and like all good cooks, she went." Whoever they are, they all know that, in the words of one of her detectives, "no matter how hard we work, she works twice as hard".

To witness a visit, or indeed a series of visits in one day (as opposed to reading a press report the next day), made by Princess Anne cannot fail to impress. It appears smooth, relaxed and beautifully orchestrated. It appears to happen as if by magic. Obviously, things can and do go wrong, but even then such problems are dealt with calmly. Her car appears at the appointed moment; Princess Anne invariably gives a polished performance. Mrs. Carew-Pole says that although there are seven of us [ladies-in-waiting] she leaves us all gasping. We flag long before she shows the slightest sign of it . . .

But the ease of the visit and the polished performance of the protagonist certainly belies the time, trouble and months of hard work that go into making the visit a success. The initial request is made to Princess Anne's private secretary and the approach is acknowledged. It is then brought up at the next planning meeting (held every six months) and the merits and demerits carefully considered. It is her decision alone, and once made, the tried and tested machinery is put into operation. A letter of acceptance is sent and a date fixed for an inspection. One of her detectives, and possibly her private secretary, then make a "recce" of the place. They time the car journey, marking off certain points on the route so that, on the day, they know if they are ahead or behind schedule and should go faster or slower. Once there, no detail is too small. They examine everything minutely. They meet, where possible, those who are to be presented. They inspect the inscription of the plaque to be unveiled; they examine the lavatory that will be put at her sole disposal. They go over the precise route that Princess Anne will make. Nothing is left to chance. Once, when visiting HMS *Eastbourne*:

the visit went like clockwork, largely because of the forethought of the squadron's anti-submarine officer, 34–year-old Lieutenant-Commander Stephen Emberton, of Plymouth. To make sure the Princess would be able to negotiate the narrow companion-ways, steep ladders and hatchways in a tight skirt, he went through a special rehearsal—in drag.

Everyone connected with the visit will be thoroughly briefed. If Princess Anne is lunching or dining (or even breakfasting, as with the opening of the new Harrods' Food Hall), they will be given notice of her likes and dislikes—no alcohol, no rich food, no long speeches. Just before a visit, the route and places are searched by the police and "sniffer" dogs. Overseas visits are planned in the same way, her staff preparing the ground months in advance. If Princess Anne is using the Andover of the Queen's Flight, as with her recent trips to Africa, the pilots will practise the take-off and landings at every destination. Often, the airports turn out to be little more than mud or sand strips.

During her visit to Australia in 1984, the press were quick to point out that Princess Anne arrived in the same dress that she had worn when last there in 1978. When Michael Parkinson put the point to her on his chat show, she merely replied with a wide grin, "Oh, it's much older than that!" Unlike the Queen Mother who refers to her clothes as her "props", Princess Anne thinks of her clothes as just part of her job. To her, they have to be practical.

> A good suit goes on forever. If it is made properly in the first place and has a sort of classic look about it, you can go on wearing it *ad infinitum*. Those are the clothes I like. There's an economic element in it. The economy is bred into me. I was brought up by my parents and by my nanny to believe that things were not to be wasted. All my childhood life. And that lesson does last, there's no question about it. I expect my clothes to last a long time.

For these "good suits", and practically all her wardrobe, Princess Anne has been going to Maureen Baker since her first public engagement in 1968. Theirs is a solid relationship, each trusting the other's judgement implicitly, and ably demonstrated when Maureen Baker was chosen to design her wedding dress (see page 103) when working for Susan Small. Often, Princess Anne will take some material—a length of silk, a piece of tweed—that she has found on her travels to be made up. Maureen Baker confirms that she "is very interested in fabrics and brings them in, sometimes with a drawing, never a picture from a magazine". That interest was certainly recognised by the British Knitwear and

Clothing Export Council who invited her to become their Honorary President in 1984. The actual mechanics of dressmaking fascinates her, often asking Mrs. Baker to "show her how a sleeve is cut". Apart from Mrs. Baker, Princess Anne patronises other designers, among them Belville Sassoon and Louis Feraud. As a very standard size 8 or 10, she can, and frequently does, buy ready-made-clothes off the peg. At home, it is jeans and a sweater and the ubiquitous corduroy hat, for both practicality and comfort.

John Boyd, a quietly-spoken Scotsman, has made her hats from the beginning. He works closely with her designers for style and fabric and again, has a strong working relationship with her. He can transform an idea or a sketch into the real thing, so much so that Princess Anne's hats have become her trademark. She has never thought of herself as a trendsetter, believing herself to be:

rather conservative. I'm not prepared to take risks. Curiously enough, I feel that as I get older I'm getting more adventuresome. But following the fashion is very restricting; if you really follow fashion, you have to get new clothes every year. And I'm not one for that. I've got clothes I've had for years, and I intend going on wearing them because I like them, I

178

liked them when I bought them and I like them now—more so perhaps.

Clothes generally look well on Princess Anne, not just because she wears them well and are well made, but she is, as far as there is such a thing, the "right shape", a supposed 35–25–37 figure, long legs and a slender neck. One of Princess Anne's best features is her hair, though she has admitted that "it is her life's work taming it!" In fact, she has always done her own hair with the very occasional help from Michael Rasser of Michaeljohn, such as putting up what is now dubbed the "Royal roll' for a State Opening of Parliament. It was he who suggested the punk-style pink streaks in her hair for the presentation of the 1984 BAFTA awards. "The Princess told me she was wearing a stunning pink dress, and I suggested that she went for something really daring and coloured two dramatic streaks in her hair to match," he said. "The Princess definitely seemed keen on the idea, and the reaction to it was fantastic." Like most members of the Royal Family, she has lovely skin and cares for it (when asked why she never exposed her face to the sun, Princess Margaret once replied, "Have you ever tried making up a saddle?").

Yet despite these natural attributes, Princess Anne does not photograph well—the most frequent comment is that she is much prettier than in her photographs. However, certain of her

179

studio portrait photographs show her in her truest light. Her uncle, Lord Snowdon, has taken excellent birthday portraits, as has the Queen Mother's favourite photographer, Norman Parkinson. Over the years, he has taken several excellent portraits of her, not least the engagement and wedding photographs. For those, he used his considerable skill as a fashion photographer and techniques to make her appear totally beautiful. One New York journalist commented that "the hoydenish sportswoman had become a spectacular bride". Parkinson also used the top make-up man, Oliver Echaud-maison from Paris, who stayed on to make her up for the wedding itself. While the world marvelled at the photographs, it was thought that the Duke of Edinburgh disapproved of them as they "made her look too pretty". Parkinson, with his charm and ebullient manner, brings out the best in subjects, Royal or commoner, and that shows in the end result. He is the archetypal Court photographer, totally at ease with his sitter. Such ease of working and dealing with Princess Anne invariably produces good results. Her local photographer in Gloucestershire, Peter Harding, enjoys that same easy working relationship as he photographs her and her family, once for their Christmas card. One year, 1978, it was of a baby Peter Phillips wearing his father's cap.

Princess Anne's public appearances are as

varied as they are numerous. Her most spectacular ones are, of course, ceremonial. There are the various State occasions throughout the year where she plays her integral part. She is seen during State visits from foreign royalty and heads of government. She is there at the banquets and the balls given in their honour, in her supportive role to the Queen. Members of the House of Lords see her seated below her parents, demurely listening to the Queen's speech at the State Opening of Parliament. Those who line the route from Buckingham Palace to the palace of Westminster wave to her as she passes in one of the State Coaches. One year they can only have been amazed when they witnessed the procession come to a standstill, as Princess Anne recalled:

something startled the horses that were pulling our carriage, and the whole thing came to a grinding halt. . . . So we got out in the middle of the Mall, and the rest of the procession disappeared up the Mall, and the other half of the procession was stuck behind us, and we were dressed, you know, in just the sort of thing you wear on a mid November morning in London, like a long white dress, a tiara and uniform, rather sort of vaguely waiting to be picked up by something or somebody. And fortunately a car did come to our rescue and we continued, followed by the procession, which was fine for us because we were in the car, but I don't think the escort behind us enjoyed themselves very much because they had to go a great deal faster than they were used to.

To the thirty thousand who go to the five annual Royal Garden parties held each year at Buckingham Palace and the Palace of Holyroodhouse in Edinburgh, there is the chance that they might catch a glimpse of her as she makes her way through the crowds. Sometimes those who are in some way connected with one of her charities or societies, are singled out by an aide to be introduced to her. There, and indeed during every visit, she makes a lasting impression on those she meets, even though they do not always recall what she says with any degree of accuracy. Princess Anne finds that

because you're "royal", anything you say might be given extra significance. You know from experience that people tend to remember —or *think* they remember—what you said. I frequently meet people for the second time, perhaps years after the first time, who say: "I remember you saying such-and-such to me", and I know at once that it wasn't me that said that—we may have been talking about that particular subject, but I just wouldn't have said that thing. The words couldn't have been mine—not the way I speak.

There are many requests for a visit by Princess Anne that are unrelated to any of the organisations, charities and branches of the Services with which she is connected (see Appendix I). She is much in demand for foreign visits, (see Appendix II) as the Queen's representative, but again, most of these trips are connected with her Service appointments or her particular charities or a combination of all three. At home, there are the usual rounds of civic visits, hospital visits and schools. There are factories of every description—she once admitted that she knew "all about Kleenex factories". In the main, however, Princess Anne's public diary is filled with engagements covering those organisations with which she has become so closely involved. More often than not, she will visit an area, taking in many varied engagements, switching from charity to commerce, from hospital to education to business all in the same day. A typical day, 3 March 1986, reported in the court circular of *The Times* read:

March 3: The Princess Anne, Mrs. Mark Phillips visited Derbyshire today.
    Having been received by Her Majesty's Lord Lieutenant for Derbyshire (Colonel Peter Hilton) Her Royal Highness, President of the

Save the Children Fund, opened the Fund's Shop in Chesterfield.

Afterwards The Princess Anne, Mrs. Mark Phillips, visited the Midland Railway Trust Station at Ripley escorted by the President and Chairman of the Trust (Mrs. K. Mew).

Her Royal Highness was later entertained to luncheon at Ilkeston Park.

The Princess Anne, Mrs. Mark Phillips, this afternoon visited Charnos Factory, Ilkeston in celebration of their Golden Jubilee and was received on arrival by the Chairman of the Directors (Mr. R. Noskwith).

Her Royal Highness later opened the new Design Block at Trent College (Headmaster Mr. A. Maltby) in Long Easton and unveiled two commemorative plaques.

Afterwards The Princess Anne, Mrs. Mark Phillips, visited Birkins Lace Factory, Borrowash and was received on arrival by the Managing Director (Mr. F. Attenborough).

Her Royal Highness, attended by the Hon. Mrs. Legge-Bourke, travelled in an aircraft of The Queen's Flight.

As head of the Army, it is the Queen who appoints the Colonel-in-Chief of her regiments, usually a member of the Royal Family. It is the regiment, however, who decides on which member of the Royal Family they would like to be their Colonel-in-Chief. As there are still more regiments in the British Army than there are members of the Royal Family, it was quick (and foresighted) of the 14th/20th King's Hussars to be the first to invite Princess Anne to become their Colonel-in-Chief in 1969. They deemed it an honour to be accepted; she became proud of her first regiment. They were even able to present her with a clever memento of the occasion in the form of a car numberplate 1420 H (14th/20th Hussars). It was found on a milk float in London by their then adjutant.

Her first visit to the regiment in Germany was an instant success. She had had experience of mess life, having frequently dined with those regiments on Royal guard duty. She also had a genuine rapport with the troopers and the non-commissioned officers—she had, of course, met some of the "jocks" (other ranks) of the Scottish regiments at Balmoral. One, Fusilier McCurdy of the Royal Highland Fusiliers, has cause never to forget her. He was riding a pony back to the Castle after a day's stalking. Princess Anne swept round the corner in her car, startled the pony, which planted the Fusilier in the heather on the roadside and ran off. Princess Anne leapt out of her car and caught the pony. She then rode it back to Balmoral, McCurdy driving her car. When they returned, the transport had already left for Ballater, so Princess Anne drove the Fusilier back to the camp to the amazement of the guard. She declined, however, his invitation for a drink in the NAAFI.

The 14th/20th Hussars were soon followed by other regiments. The infantry regiment, the Worcestershire and Sherwood Foresters (29th/45th Foot), asked her to be their Colonel-in-Chief in the same year of their amalgamation. Commonwealth regiments asked for her too, the 8th Canadian Hussars (Princess Louise's) being the first. When she added the Royal Corps of Signals to the list, she inherited its sister regiments in Canada, Australia and New Zealand together with their benevolent institutions. She is also Colonel-in-Chief of the Royal Scots Regiment (the Royal Regiment).

On her many visits to her regiments, Princess Anne generally divides the off-duty time between the officers and the non-commissioned officers, the other ranks and, of course, all their wives. For example, when she visited the 14th/20th Hussars in Germany in February 1985, her first engagement was tea in the sergeants' mess where she moved from table to table, and so met the majority of the Wives' Club. On that three-day visit, she lunched on both days in the sergeants' mess (one recorded in their regimental magazine as a "sumptuous compo-based feast of mulligatawny soup, beefburger in pastry, and peaches in chocolate sauce") dined twice with the officers —on the first night with the Colonel of the Regiment, Lieutenant-Colonel Smales, with whom she was staying, and the next night with the officers in their mess. The officers have always thought her a "good sport, for even though she only drinks Coke, she always joins in with the regimental tradition of "drinking the health of the Emperor", in champagne from a large silver chamber pot. The chamber pot was captured by the 14th Light Dragoons from King Joseph of Spain's carriage (a present from his brother, the Emperor Napoleon) after the Battle of Vittoria, 1813. It is known today as "the Emperor" and the Regiment still enjoys its nickname of "The Emperor's Chambermaids".

But Princess Anne does more than chat to troopers' wives and drink champagne from potties on her visits to the regiment. A visit from their Colonel-in-Chief does much for their morale, particularly if they are on manoeuvres, whether it be Salisbury Plain, Catterick or the wilds of Saltau in West Germany. Apart from sharpening up the officers and men, her presence in the field gives an extra dimension to any exercise. It becomes special, where they can demonstrate their operational readiness to defend Queen and country to the Queen's personal representative.

On manoeuvres, Princess Anne is ever practical, dressing sensibly for the part. In Germany with the 14th/20th, she wore (according to the magazine again) "a sharply pressed green denim creation from the latest MOD Bicester collection, including name tags, webbing belt and Dior head scarf," with the pips of a full colonel on her epaulettes. She takes a genuine interest in all things mechanical, spending hours peering into engines, the bodies of tanks and armoured cars. She is shown the latest sophisticated communications systems and has enough knowledge to ask intelligent questions. To the delight of the Hussars, not to say the press, she has driven their fifty-six-ton Chieftain tanks across rough ground at fifty miles an hour as well as their smaller Scorpion tanks; with the Worcestershire and Sherwood Foresters she has driven their new twenty-four-ton armoured personnel carrier. She even understands the rudiments of their weaponry, indulgent sergeants barking a full six-week course in fifteen minutes at her in deep regimental growls. It is always good when the Colonel-in-Chief scores a direct hit with everything from a sten-gun to Chieftain tank. During the 1985 visit to the 14th/20th Hussars in Germany:

The Princess had never fired a Chieftain before, so it was a particularly special occasion. [The tank crew] performed an expert demonstration before dismounting and meeting the Princess. . . . The Princess acquitted herself splendidly, achieving first-round hits with DST [Discarding Sabot] at ranges out to 2,500 metres.

Firing live HESH [High Explosive Squash Head] she lifted the turret of one target into the air for some distance. As a finale, she fired HESH at a range of 3,000 metres, where she achieved a second-round hit—overall, a very impressive performance from our Colonel-in-Chief.

Princess Anne's regiments know that she cares deeply for them all. She is proud of their respective histories and traditions, and as knowledgeable as any in the regiment. She tries to visit each one at least once a year, and will always make sure that she is kept informed of all regimental news.

It is inevitable that, with her interest in servicemen and their wives, coupled with her genuine, caring nature, Princess Anne should be asked to be patron of related charities connected with their welfare. She is a life member of the Royal British Legion Women's Section. She is also Patron of the Royal Tournament.

Although the majority of her work with the Services is with the Army, Princess Anne is also an Honorary Air Commodore of RAF Lynham in Wiltshire, one of the airfields that she uses when she travels by the Queen's Flight. It is, however, with the Senior Service (the Navy) that the Royal Family have been most closely associated for the past six generations, from the Sailor King, William IV, to Prince Andrew. Princess Anne, too, would like to have joined the Royal Navy, saying that she is

a nautical person at heart. Maybe it runs in the blood a bit. I think any kind of sea-going life would appeal to me. If I'd been born a boy, I would like to have gone to sea. . . . The problem is that I get sea-sick. It normally wears off, it depends how long I'm given to get my sea-legs. Perhaps if I had gone to sea as a job, it would have worn off. [There are] not too many opportunities for women to work at sea.

Thus, she was a good choice when the Queen appointed her Chief Commandant of the Women's Royal Naval Services in July 1974. In true Princess Anne fashion, she is no titular head of that arm of the Service, but takes a keen interest in their work and their welfare. As a former army wife, she can appreciate the problems of Service life, and that, coupled with a life-long interest and knowledge of the Royal Navy, made her appointment popular with the serving officers and ratings.

Another "sea-post" that Princess Anne holds is President of the Missions to Seamen. When a seafarer was asked what the Missions meant to him, he replied simply, "They're just there." "Being there" to the million and a half seamen means a welcome in over three hundred ports around the world, a friendly ear and pastoral counselling, and a link with home. Despite the number of organisations she actively works for, now over seventy, Princess Anne can still speak knowledgeably on the inner workings of each. When asked in September 1985 about the Mission's work on Radio 4's *Tuesday Call*, her reply was spontaneous, well informed and accurate, despite the fact that she has been President only since 1983. As with all her charities, her knowledge is gained at first hand, by talking to the staff and members. When she visited their centre in Dubai, she spoke to forty seamen, some the victims of the Gulf War. She has seen their workings in East Africa, visiting their centre in Dar-es-Salaam. No trouble is too great, she even broke her journey from Australia in 1983 to open a new Mission club in Singapore. Preaching at the service when she was installed as their President, the general secretary, Bill Down, said that the "Mission was facing a time of change and that it was a growing and expanding society. We are moving into the future with Your Royal Highness at our head. No society could ask for a more hard-working president or dedicated ambassadress." Canon Down was correct. Apart from seeing and meeting the voluntary staff in the field, she reads their reports and attends their meetings. At their Annual General Meeting, while praising their work, she was not above giving them a school-mistressy pep-talk: "There is no room for complacency. When the going gets tough, it is time for the committed to stand up and be counted . . . can you see to it, that by this time next year the membership in the country is double." In return, those who work for the Missions to Seamen are truly impressed by her energy and the effect their Royal President has had on their organisation.

On the same radio programme, Princess Anne spoke of another of her roles as Commandant-in-Chief of the St. John Ambulance and Nursing Cadets. There she admitted that, although she was never a nursing cadet herself, she did at least similar first-aid exams at school. Over the years she has of course been able to see the work of the nursing cadets in the field, not least attending various horse trials throughout her competitive career. "During the course of the year, I normally attend one or two major cadet functions, and possibly several fund raising functions for the St. Johns," she said on *Tuesday Call*. Every organiser knows what a Royal presence, particularly Princess Anne, can do to a charity ball. After she attended a performance in aid of one of her lesser-known charities, the Home Farm Trust that cares for the adult handicapped, their director John Woodcock said of her, "To put it bluntly, we got front-page coverage with a picture of the Princess in the *Sunday Telegraph Magazine*, and with her London Paladium show attendance, we trebled the money we had made with any other single event."

Princess Anne has become the obvious choice to fill the vacancy of a new patron or president. Charity committees know only too well that her contribution will be so much more than just lending her name. Thus, when Lord Rupert Nevill died, Princess Anne took over in April 1983 as the President of the British Olympic Association. As a former Olympic competitor, she was the obvious choice. What the committee did not foresee was just how successful their choice would prove to be, and how hard she worked for the Association and each British Olympic competitor. After all, she knows only too well what it means to be selected to compete. She has said:

If only those in authority realised what it means to a sportsman to train for four years and then to be told that they cannot go, they wouldn't be so fast to make decisions that can totally destroy someone's hopes. There is nothing like an Olympic Games; I know, I've been, and I want everyone who is capable of winning a place to be able to go. That's why I am willing to go anywhere and meet anyone to try and raise the funds for our athletes.

True to her word, as always, Princess Anne travelled all over the country raising money for the Association. In early 1984, she flew to

Houston for the start of her fund-raising tour of the United States. The fabulously oil-rich and the not so rich flocked to meet her, paying anything between $50 for a small reception to $1,500 for a dinner at the Petroleum Club. One billionaire stated that the "evening has cost me $20,000 all told, but honey, you're worth every red cent". The impressive four-day tour, which took in twenty-four engagements over twelve thousand miles, raised $70,000. It was a great coup to get the Americans to part with their money so willingly so that another nation could compete against them.

Princess Anne was there too at the 1984 Winter Olympics at Sarajevo, Yugoslavia, in her role as president of the British Olympic Association to witness Torvill and Dean win their gold medals, and returned to the United States for the main Olympics, held that year in Los Angeles. Over seventeen days, she met the whole of that British squad, often watching them competing. The press made more of the fact that she stayed in a different hotel to her husband than the contribution she made to the British team. It was left to Zola Budd, the South African-born runner, and her flowing Olympic diary in the *Daily Mail* to put the competitors view of their President:

Today I met Princess Anne, and what a lovely person she is.
I had always thought that royalty would be

a bit remote but she was so friendly. She spent all morning with the athletes and officials who are still at the training camp in San Diego.

She spent time with us in the house where we are living, ate with us and even came to the training track with us. I had quite a long talk with her.

She was telling me all about her own Olympic experiences in 1976 when she was a member of the British Equestrian team in Montreal. She knew exactly how we are all feeling at the moment, the excitement and the worry. She promised me that it is all forgotten the moment the competition starts.

. . . It was like meeting someone you have known for years, rather than a member of the Royal Family. She really put us at our ease.

Princess Anne saw them all again when they finally made it to the Olympic village, which she described as "a hive of happiness, and well fed. In my travels around the world I find that when people are well fed that is 99 per cent of the battle."

One of the many great advantages of having Princess Anne as a President is that when she speaks, people listen. The International Olympic Committee was "strongly reminded" that the "opening ceremony should be for the benefit of the competitors", and that it was disgraceful that the athletes should have been left outside the

Olympic Stadium while the ceremony was staged for the benefit of television. She also spoke out forcibly at events held "at ludicrously inappropriate times, and often in dangerous temperatures for the benefit of prime-time American television". Preparing for the 1988 Olympics to be held in Seoul, South Korea, Princess Anne is in the same battling mood for the British squad.

It is not for nothing, with her Mountbatten forebears, that Princess Anne is a born tactician. For some, like the International Olympic Committee, it is the head-banging and flag-waving approach that is needed to produce results. More often, however, it is Princess Anne's gentle, quiet approach that no one can refuse that works better. It is, however, that approach, combined with the genuinely worthy cause that is unbeatable, whether it be for money, voluntary help, publicity or "just getting things done". Everyone, in every organisation that Princess Anne is involved with, knows only too well what having her support means to their organisation—when she was asked to attend a concert in aid of the Home Farm Trust, she agreed but said that she "would much rather go to any of the homes and meet the people involved". The public rarely sees this side of her, only "the tip of the iceberg" that she does for her two main charities, Riding for the Disabled and the now world-famous Save the Children Fund.

It made a great deal of sense that, being a member of the Royal Family *and* one of the best-known equestriennes in the country, that Princess Anne should be asked to become the Patron of the Riding for the Disabled Association. The invitation came from their President, Lavinia, Duchess of Norfolk, who thought that, considering the amount of work she put into the charity, their roles should be reversed and now Princess Anne is President, the Duchess Patron. In fact, as one of their voluntary helpers explained, "they both work extremely hard for the charity".

The Riding for the Disabled Association was formed in 1969 out of the Advisory Council for the Disabled. Today, there are nearly six hundred groups that cater for nearly twenty thousand children and adults with physical and mental disabilities. To them, riding comes as a new challenge that

often brings rewards of improved co-ordination and balance, a feeling of independence, greater self-confidence and a resulting happiness. Newly found capabilities begin to take precedence over long-accepted disabilities. New human relationships develop with the voluntary helpers of the Association, often the first step from a sheltered life at home or the professional environment of special school or hospital into the world outside.

Princess Anne admits that, in common with all her other charities, such patronage does give her a wonderful opportunity to meet people. As she says, she had

always ridden and had a lot of pleasure from my association with equestrian sports, and in fact, there is an extraordinary ability for the disabled to enjoy the same things, through I think the connection with the animals.

Formerly, members of the Royal Family accepted every patronage that was offered, as it was thought rude to turn anyone down. Today, they are more than just figureheads with a passing interest in the organization, none more so than Princess Anne. Her contribution to the Riding for the Disabled Association goes further than just asking favours of potential benefactors. "Princess Anne has a way of getting people to donate money and other gifts to charity which, in anyone else, would seem blatant," Lavinia, Duchess of Norfolk once said. Her knowledge of the Association and its inner working coupled with her understanding of the disabled and the horses make her a key figure in its success.

Her involvement with the RDA in 1985 was typical of her contribution to the charity. She received the 8th Jubilee Saddle at a lunch for the Council at the Saddlers' Hall, presented by the Worshipful Company of Saddlers (she is also a Yeoman of the Saddlers' Company). She attended the charity preview of *Guys and Dolls* given in aid of the Variety Club of Great Britain and the Association, and the Christmas Olympia Show in December. She rode in the Charity race at Sandown, (page 74) and in a sponsored ride at Badminton. On top of that, she visited eight RDA centres, from the Glenfarg Group in Perthshire to the Diptford Group in Devon, from the Enniskillen Group in Northern Ireland to the Hadleigh Group in Suffolk.

It is with these visits to the groups that Princess Anne's personal contribution to the Association is most marked. For instance, when she visited the Cranleigh Group of Surrey officially to open their new stables, she spoke to every single person there that day, nearly four hundred people. She presented each child with a badge to mark the occasion, talking to each one, instantly recognising their disability and tempering her conversation to each. Her conversations with each of the helpers gave encouragement and pleasure. Later, when it was mentioned that a group in Sussex were having difficulty in finding helpers, one suggested that "they should send Princess Anne down there, then they would be snowed under with help". In fact, during that visit, her whole entourage took part as well, her lady-in-waiting that day, Mrs. Malcolm Innes joining in, while the pilot of the Wessex of the Queen's Flight made quick sketches of the children and the helicopter. Princess Anne enjoys these visits too; she will remember a particular pony from years before, as well as the regular helpers. She is very good with the disabled, apparently not minding how badly disabled or autistic they are—she told Brian Hoey that she supposed that it was all part of her training. "It's not only important for the person concerned, but perhaps even more so for the parents who may be standing nearby. It would be terribly hurtful if one stepped backwards just to avoid someone dribbling over you."

Every year, Princess Anne attends the Association's Annual General Meeting, not just as a figurehead but as a working member of Council. One of the helpers admits to being partisan when speaking about Princess Anne. She recalled the 1985 AGM with the President, Lavinia, Duchess of Norfolk—"a shock of red hair and wild gesticulation with her hands' —making her speech, followed by Princess Anne, who

> spoke without a note for twenty minutes, amplifying each of the Duchess's points with the precision and clarity of one who really knows what she is talking about. When not actually engaged in serious business, there was a continual, really witty exchange between

them. With Princess Anne at the helm, no wonder Riding for the Disabled is such a success.

Those able children appreciate the Patron of their Association too. When Princess Anne presented a little girl with her commemorative badge, she exclaimed, "Oh God!" "Not quite," replied Princess Anne.

Princess Anne is a person of extraordinary energy and diverse talents. Much of her time is spent helping the underprivileged and bolstering the talented, but there is another facet to her eclectic collection of roles, and that is the quasi-academic position of Chancellor of the University of London.

The Federal University of London is by far the largest of Britain's universities with over fifty faculties and forty-two thousand students, many from overseas. At the beginning of the nine-teenth century, the only universities were Oxford and Cambridge, whose undergraduates were almost all the sons of the rich or members of the Church of England. In 1836 a Royal Charter was granted to the new University of London "to hold forth to all classes and denominations . . . without any distinction whatsoever an encourage-ment for pursuing a regular and liberal course of education". The same liberal standards prevailed —women were admitted to study in 1862, later, in 1888, as one Victorian witness delicately put it, the first four "sweet girl-graduates in their gold-hair" were granted their degrees. They appointed the first woman Vice-Chancellor, Dame Lillian Penson, but even more significant, they were the first university to appoint a woman Chancellor, Queen Elizabeth the Queen Mother in 1955.

The appointment of Chancellor is for life, but after nearly thirty years of devoted service the Queen Mother stood down. By that time, her successor had to be elected by the members of convocation (the representative graduate body) rather than appointed and, after the Queen Mother suggested her grand-daughter, "a sounding was taken around the university" as to how another Royal Chancellor would be received. When found favourable, her name, along with the Transport and General Workers Union retired leader, the late Jack Jones, and the jailed African Nationalist leader, Nelson Mandela, was put forward. Although at that time, Princess Anne was not enjoying the best of press, she was elected with a resounding majority polling over twice and three times as many votes as her rivals. Before she was enrolled as Chancellor on 17 February 1981, she was offered an honorary degree but, to her credit, she declined saying that it was better that they should wait and see how she fared.

As Chancellor she is the head of the university, but her functions are largely ceremonial, leaving

202

the Vice-Chancellor free to run the academic and business sides of the university. The fact that she is Chancellor of a university and has never attended one does not worry her. Nor does she feel intimidated by the accademic world. She believes that "one of the things that you have to learn early on in our sort of life is not to feel inadequate, because you certainly don't know half as much as they [the academics] do, but you can always learn".

The majority of her job as Chancellor is ceremonial, Princess Anne hooding those chosen for Honorary Degrees once a year, presiding over the presentation ceremony three or four times a year, when fifteen hundred to two thousand graduates bow or curtsey to her at the Royal Albert Hall, and attending dinners for benefactors or for retiring dignitaries. In their 150th year, 1986, she even named a train, the "University of London". Like the former Chancellor, Princess Anne is especially interested in people, from overseas, often visiting the Lillian Pension Hall of residence for foreign students. She attends various of the Student Union functions and the Purple Dinners (the equivalent of a blue at Oxbridge).

The University of London has a very wide range of faculties, many of them scientific and medical. Where those members of the faculties appreciate visits from their Chancellor, Princess Anne enjoys a visit to them. When she visits the

London School of Hygiene and Tropical Medicine, she can discuss malaria and tropical diseases with the knowledge of one who has seen the problems for herself in the field; at a visit to an exhibition on child welfare at the Institute of Child Health, she can speak as one who has studied the problems first-hand. She knows only too well (from expensive experience with her own horses) what is going on at the Royal Veterinary College.

Over the year, Princess Anne attends about fifteen separate functions to do with her university—more during the 150–year celebrations. She takes great interest in the developments and is popular with undergraduates and staff alike, one declaring, "She is very good to work with and extremely energetic."

Once a member of the Royal Family has taken an institution to heart, then it is theirs for life, or until they hand over to another (generally to a younger member of the family). In the case of the British Academy of Film and Television Arts (BAFTA), it was their penultimate president, Lord Louis Mountbatten, who "bequeathed" the presidency to his great-niece, Princess Anne. With his son-in-law, Lord Brabourne, they were involved in setting up the association at 195 Piccadilly with the money, £60,000, donated by the Queen, from her share of the proceeds of the film *Royal Family*. Its aims are:

to promote, maintain, improve, and advance original and creative work among persons engaged in film and television production; to create and maintain a high standard of qualification and performance in such persons; and to encourage and promote experiment and research in the arts, sciences, and techniques of film and television production.

A very busy life precludes watching much television and cinema viewing for Princess Anne although the Royal Family indent for video recordings of their favourite programmes and series from the BBC and ITV for their Christmas viewing at Windsor and Sandringham. Also, like the Queen, she occasionally slips into the back of a cinema to watch a film after the lights have gone down. BAFTA's director, Reginald Collin, cannot overrate Princess Anne's contribution to the organisation. Where she adds glamour to even the most star-studded occasions, she will also turn out for the unglamourous technicians' awards.

Nothing is too much trouble or too hard, as Mr. Collin recalls:

You should have seen her promoting British films and Television in Los Angeles last July [1984]. We started at 8 a.m. and finished at 1 a.m. the next morning. That was seventeen hours, eight engagements and two speeches on our feet and sometimes we would sit down for a minute and she'd say, "What! Not getting tired, surely?"

9

Saving the Children

THERE are two distinct pictures of Princess Anne on duty. The one is neat, tidy and smartly dressed, often with a hat, sometimes gloves as well. The other is casual, a light check cotton blouse, denim skirt, headscarf and rubber-soled desert boots. According to the Hon. Shân Legge-Bourke, Princess Anne buys her desert boots in the Scout Shop in Buckingham Palace Road, "the best you'll find in London". What is common to these two images, however, is the brooch. It is a particularly stylish, enamel brooch of three international signalling flags that spell out SCF with the Save the Children Fund flag on the top.

Princess Anne was invited to become their president in 1970 on the retirement of Viscount Boyd of Merton, the former Colonial Secretary. From her point of view, the choice was a personal one, although she admitted that she "did not know why the Save the Children Fund had asked me to become President, but they did, and it was down to me to say yes or no." In a very early film, *The Princess and the Children*, she revealed the reasons behind accepting her new role:

I think what really decided me to accept the Presidency of the Save the Children Fund was that I'd had quite a few invitations to become patron of various institutions, and I think "Patron" is a frightfully vague office and that the office of "President" gives the idea of doing something more definite. I don't think children really came into my original thoughts about it, not necessarily because I like children —if you've got two small brothers that isn't the first thing that enters your head, but I think it is a tremendous work to do because they are a very important age-group and they need a lot more help then than possibly later. If they can get a good start, it is very encouraging for them. I hope I have accepted it for the right reasons.

Ten years later, as a mother, she amplified her original thoughts when she admitted that it was not just a matter of being interested in children, but investing in the future.

If you don't invest in people at the earliest point of their lives, you miss an opportunity. And you never get the chance again. It's not just a matter of helping to look after children to see that they have a decent upbringing so that they don't grow up contributing to more violence, more crime. What you are really after, the basic thing, is to give them a chance of survival—relatively healthy survival.

The Save the Children Fund was Princess Anne's first major challenge in life and consequently, she has made it very much her life's work. She said she knew nothing about voluntary work when she started, "beyond having sponsored a child through the Fund when I was at school and visting the elderly through the Girl Guides". She immersed herself in its workings, learning by experience both in the field and in the committee room, at home and abroad. She has been well taught, invariably "impressed with the projects and always with the professionalism of the staff who are practical, positive, full of common sense and not prone to panic in a crisis"—qualities that seem to apply to the President herself.

She is thoroughly at home at every level of the organisation, from the role of the Director-General down to the humblest voluntary helper at a jumble sale or coffee morning. As far as the Fund is concerned, she is a working president first, a member of the Royal Family second. She can represent them at any level and negotiate on their behalf. In March 1986, she put the Fund's position to the governmental body that co-ordinates overseas aid (Overseas Development Association). Also, being a member of the Royal

Family *and* the working president, she has that extra authority when dealing with heads of governments abroad and integrating their programmes with the respective country. Princess Anne is keen to explain the workings of the Fund, especially abroad where they

are not offering high-tech, high-octane help but something more basic which it can be easy for Western-based agencies to miss out. The point abroad is the same as here, in the final analysis, community involvement.

For instance, in the West African areas I visited on my recent trips, the Fund had gone round the villagers, getting the elders to pick both a village health worker and a birth attendant—mid-wife is too technical a term— whom the Fund will train in simple health care.

Thus the community has an interest in the scheme's success; it is not being imposed on them from outside. That can be the problem of more technical aid. Too many moving parts is a frequent objection because not only do the local people not have the expertise to maintain things but tropical climates lead to frequent breakdowns.

In her years as President of Save the Children Fund, Princess Anne has visited every continent where the Fund operates, and some countries more than once. If there is the remotest prospect of visiting a Save the Children project when on some other engagement, she is certain to combine the two. When she visited the 14th/20th King's Hussars in Hong Kong in 1971, she divided her time between the regiment and the Fund. She laid a foundation stone for a new hospital, visited the Wong Tai Sin Rehabilitation Centre and the Tung Wah Hospital. She visited fisherwomen and their families supported by the Fund. Sometimes Princess Anne's visits produce results unwittingly. A remote village on the Sai Kung Peninsular had been petitioning for years for a fresh water supply. As soon as it was rumoured that Princess Anne might visit the village, a pipe-line was instantly laid to Hang Hau.

For Princess Anne to stay in the luxury of Government House and sample the delights of a cavalry mess and a four-star hotel is indeed rare with any overseas tour of the Save the Children Fund. More often, she is experiencing acute discomfort, primitive conditions and strenuous travel, even sickness. Before visiting Third World countries, she is innoculated against cholera, hepatitis, meningitis, yellow fever, typhoid, tetanus, rabies. On her first visit abroad for the Fund in 1973 to Ethiopia, she had what a Buckingham Palace spokesman called "a minor stomach upset" after a three-day mule trek to the Simeon Mountains. It was not surprising that

211

she should have been struck by something after the intense heat and squalor of some of the places she visited.

After a gap of eight years, Princess Anne began what has become her annual, sometimes bi-annual, tours on behalf of the Fund. In 1981 she went to Nepal, 1982 saw her marathon trip to Africa. A visit to Pakistan in 1983 was followed by West Africa in 1984, Bangladesh and India, and Africa again the year after and Tanzania, Zambia, Mozambique and the Sudan in mid-November 1985. They were all lean trips, to arid and desolate parts of the world, that is apart from Nepal, where she stayed with the King and Queen, visited the headquarters of the Nepalese Children's Organisation in Patan, climbed up to Dhankutu to visit a mother-and-child health clinic and saw a tiger kill a young buffalo bait.

The work and effort that Princess Anne put into the Fund largely went unrecorded until her 1982 tour of six African countries. She flew by scheduled flight to Johannesburg, South Africa, where she remained in the transit lounge of the airport and assiduously ignored an invitation from the Transvaal Administrator to "come back and visit us properly next time". Princess Anne was travelling by the Andover of the Queen's Flight, funded through the Foreign Office, who pay the basic costs provided she fulfils a number of engagements other than for Save the Children

Fund on the way. She then flew on to Swaziland. The country was in mourning for its king, Sobhuza II, so it became a "low-key" visit. Princess Anne visited schools and open-air clinics to witness the start of the STOP campaign, the mass anti-polio immunisation campaign. She met the Fund workers and toured the whole kingdom which is "about the size of Surrey". In Zimbabwe she visited more clinics, including one deep in the bush, the Jairos Jiri centre for severely handicapped children. It was not all hard work, for she was able to fly up to the Victoria Falls and to see some of the wildlife from a boat on the Zambezi.

By this time, the press corps that followed her thought that it was just a pleasant trip. From then on, the pace hotted up. Dr. Hastings Banda welcomed her to Malawi and again, she was off into the bush to visit Save the Children Fund centres and to see the Flying Doctor service in action. When she and the Prince of Wales visited Kenya in 1970, she was intervieived by Valerie Singleton of BBC's *Blue Peter* and filmed when being shown round the Statehe Boys' School in Nairobi by the head boy. When she returned twelve years later, the same head-boy met her, with his wife and children, as headmaster. While staying at Diani Beach, twenty miles south of Mombasa, Princess Anne received an urgent communiqué from the Foreign Office to say that it was unsafe for her to go on to Somalia as the

213

sporadic border war with Ethiopia had flared up again. Francis Pym, the Foreign Secretary, had not bargained for Princess Anne's tenacity. She insisted ("Damn them", she is reported as saying, "I'm going"), and the tour proceeded as planned to the Boroma refugee camp. There she saw the plight of the forty thousand refugees of the war and the drought and spoke to each of the Fund workers, a visit that Princess Anne described in restrospect as "the highlight of my tour".

From there, she flew to North Yemen where she was expected to fly home direct to England but, to everyone's surprise (except those that knew her), she landed in Beirut. She spent ten hours in the city, visiting the Save the Children Fund clinic, talking to the workers, and seeing for herself the ravages of the war. With truly British understatement, the Buckingham Palace spokesman said, "What she is doing is fairly dangerous." When she returned to England, she was as usual modest of her achievement. Not so the then Director-General of the Fund, John Cumber:

> Her commitment to her job sometimes comes as a surprise to people. Unless they've met her, our people don't know what to expect, and tend to pitch the explanations of their work at the sort of level any layman can understand. But she knows her stuff all right and

they find that they have to pitch it at a much higher level.

The press and the public too were impressed with the "smiling safari" and "their Princess". The next year, 1983, when she visited the Fund's projects in Pakistan on her way home from Tokyo, the tour received serious press coverage. Television news crews were there when she toured the Afghani refugee camps. Trevor McDonald, in a highly intelligent and searching interview, brought out just how good a spokeswoman for the work of the Save the Children Fund she was, and she showed just how quickly she had grasped the social and policital problems of Pakistan and the Afghani refugees at that time. When he said that she seemed to thrive on these tours, she replied that she found them "very interesting. They do give me a chance to travel extensively in parts of a country that one wouldn't otherwise have seen which, for me, is a great advantage."

The trip to West Africa that Princess Anne made in February 1984 was especially to see the work of the Fund in the Gambia and Burkino Fasso (formerly the Upper Volta). With two extremes of climate, she flew from the snows of the Winter Olympics at Sarajevo, Yugoslavia to the heat of Morocco, where she visited a school for polio victims at Khemisset. To commemorate the occasion, the Government had presented a pair of calipers to the school. When they did not arrive, she was asked her reaction. She merely replied:

Guess . . . You just can't march in and bang your fist on the table and say this is no good and demand that things are done quickly, otherwise you would not stay in the place too long.

Four years ago, we tried to send in a team to try to fight against polio, and they were turned away. You just have to go on trying again and again. Now we run a school there, and every pupil in it is a polio victim. We do make progress.

From there she went on to the Gambia for a four-day visit. There was some political mileage to be had for President Jawara as she attended the Independence Day celebrations while he, in turn, praised the work of the Fund. Festivities over, Princess Anne then travelled up the River Gambia to Georgetown, visiting a leper colony on the way. It was a compassionate image that appeared on the news that night, when one old leper, "pathetically held out his withered stumps that were once his arms and hands and said, 'Glory to God that you have come to see us. Thank you, Princess Anne.'"

When she landed at Ouagadouggou airport, Burkino Fasso, the Andover of the Queen's

Flight had to park beside Colonel Gadaffi's private jet on the runway, but, as always, Princess Anne was above politics and the Colonel was not in evidence. It was a cool Princess Anne in a bright yellow dress and straw boater that met the new leader, Comrade President Sankhara in his camouflage jacket, revolver and jungle-boots. They spoke for half an hour, in French, on the work of the Fund in drought-stricken areas to the north of the country. The next day, she was there herself to see the famine, the malnutrition and the desperate plight of the people. One of the first helpers she met was Abdullay Barry, a Burkino Fasso relief worker with the American branch of Save the Children Fund. Standing in the middle of a cluster of mud huts at Jonga Village in temperatures that reached 115 degrees, he couldn't believe it.

I thought it would be just another public relations exercise. Instead, I was grilled in minute detail by somebody who knew exactly what she was talking about. . . . I was doing the translations, showing her the medications we used, and introducing the local child-healthcare workers. "Okay", said the Princess, "this girl is supposed to attend childbirths, just how many has she attended and what experience has she had?"

That was the first of many questions about the work, going into more and more detail.

217

It was a particularly arduous tour. There was the intense heat, the flies, the choking dust and the long drives in the Fund's Land Rover (bearing her personal standard) to outlying posts. None of it, not even the bites on her bare arms and legs, seemed to worry her. Even if they had no idea who she was, they were all glad to see her. But Princess Anne has a realistic view of their problem:

Appeals are not the answer. There are a lot of relief agencies here already. What's really needed is organisation and transport. At the end of the day, the real answer is in the hands of the *Bon Dieu*, we need Him to send us rain. I am sure that the people out here are praying to God, or whichever God they believe in, and are doing everything they can to attract his attention.

Again, Princess Anne received much publicity for the Fund and praise for herself, not least from the satirist Auberon Waugh in his *Diary*:

So. Princess Anne now emerges as a cross between Mother Teresa and Grace Kelly. I don't care. In this tiny corner she will be preserved for the nation as the Princess Anne we always knew and loved, whose poisonous spittle could stop a camel in its tracks at

218

twenty paces and blind a press photographer for life at twice the distance.

When the Queen visited the Save the Children Fund clinic in Dhaka, Bangladesh, on her tour in 1983, she saw a small child, still gaunt with hunger. She promised to tell her daughter about it and encourage her to visit the clinic. Almost a year later to the day, Princess Anne was at the clinic and met the same child, recovered and healthy. She also saw the start of a new nutrition centre, the Townswomen's Guild (of which she is Patron), funded with £750,000. The tour continued to India but was sadly cut short by the assassination of the Prime Minister, Mrs. Indira Gandhi. Two days later, she was standing beside Mrs. Thatcher at her funeral in Delhi. She completed her tour of India in February the next year.

Never still for too long, she returned to Africa at the end of 1985, the year of Band Aid and the tour of Bob Geldof across Africa. Where Geldof made a huge one-off splash and a great contribution, Princess Anne has been working steadily, and will continue to work, in her own quiet way, for the future. The present Director-General, Nicholas Hinton, says of her:

Not every African statesman has necessarily heard of SCF. But if Princess Anne is coming to his territory, you can bet your boots that he will know about it by the time she has gone. She does not shrink from asking pointed and direct questions to put local politicians on the spot.

When the *Mtoto ya Queenie*, (Swahili for the Daughter of the Queen) returned to Africa, her gruelling schedule was just what she had come to expect—no more, no less:

TANZANIA (17 November 1985)
Sunday: leave London
Monday: arrive Dar-es-Salaam
Tuesday: fly to Mbeya, visit hospitals
Wednesday: visit rehabilitation centre, fly to Songea
Thursday: fly to Zanzibar, visit hospital
Friday: view wild life Ngorongoro crater

MOZAMBIQUE (23 November 1985)
Saturday: fly to Maputo
Sunday: fly to Inhambane, visit SCF projects
Monday: Maputo hospital visits
Tuesday: visit Quelimane, leave for Lusaka

ZAMBIA (26 November 1985)
Wednesday: visit Cheshire Home and hospital
Thursday: fly to Mwinilunga to visit hospital
Friday: fly to Chipata, visit hospital; fly to copper belt
Saturday: visit copper mine, return to Lusaka

Sunday: return to Dar-es-Salaam
SUDAN (2 December 1985)
Monday: arrive Khartoum
Tuesday: visit hospital
Wednesday: fly to Niyala, visit SCF work-shops
Thursday: fly and drive to Umbala camp
Friday: drive to Zalingei; return to Khartoum
Saturday: fly to Gedaref, visit camps
Sunday: return to Khartoum
Monday: visit War Cemetery, return to London (9 December)

When Princess Anne goes to visit any project of the Save the Children Fund, she is shown what she wants to see, not what someone else thinks that she ought to see, however distressing. She has had to come to terms with the smell of death, disease and despair:

I don't find that a major problem when I visit those sort of places. It's partly because when you're there and you've seen the normal conditions in rural areas, you've become accustomed to that level of expectancy. It is much more difficult to gauge it when you are sitting in your comfortable home, in front of either a television set or listening to the radio, and you're surrounded by hot and cold running water, and electric light and all the things that we take for granted. In many of these places, the people are happy with what they have. To some extent, it is their normal way of life, and a very healthy one too. They are happy with it and their expectancy of how to cope with the lack of water is very good. But obviously there are moments when their conditions get worse, but again, it's not as if it were something out of the blue or completely new to them. Many of them have experienced it before. So it's easier to look at what you're seeing from a practical point of view, in terms of how you're going to constructively help those who are suffering, and what you can do to stop it happening quite so badly again. There are many of those climatic conditions which produce disasters, which obviously you will never be able to do anything about, but you can at least produce a system or a way of approaching the problem that will make it easier in the future. When you're there and actually seeing children who are severely malnourished, possibly on the point of dying, it's never a sight that anybody really wants to see, but I think you are involved in the business of actually trying to help.

There are no frills attached to these tours, no red carpets, just as there are no frills at the refugee camps. When asked about such things as washing, her lady-in-waiting, the Hon. Shân Legge-Bourke, who often accompanies her, says, "We just stand under the shower with our clothes on—if there is a shower. But a bucket will do." When she stays at a refugee camp, she neither receives nor expects any special treatment for her Royal status, save possibly for her own chemical thunder-box. She sleeps in the same huts, is bitten by the same bedbugs "little 'friends' who shared my sleeping bag" as she calls them. She eats the same food. Mark Bowden, who co-ordinates the whole of the African campaign, says:

There is a communal kitchen where the local staff prepare food that is either tinned, dried or heavily dominated by the only meat available—goat. There is goat stew, goat spaghetti bolognese, and goat everything you can think of. . . . She [Princess Anne] is the most marvellous person who makes the most difficult conditions fun. Her presence gives everyone an enormous boost.

Those who travel with Princess Anne on her trips all confirm that she is a marvellous travelling companion, witty, and with a great capacity to relieve tension. At one dusty airstrip, she peered out of the window of the Andover to see the guard of honour with its captain standing to rigid attention awaiting the Royal guest. According to Alan Hamilton of *The Times*:

"Good God!" exclaimed the President of the

223

Save the Children Fund, more in mirth than horror, "his flies are undone!" The official greeting, moments later, was strictly eye-to-eye.

Travel itself can be hazardous, or at least unnerving. During a tour, the greatest distances are covered by an Andover of the Queen's Flight, but even there, travel can be alarming. When Princess Anne arrived at Goram Goram, in Burkino Fasso, the airstrip was indistinguishable from the rest of the Sahara desert, with no control tower, radio or fire extinguishers. However, the authorities did manage to find a fire engine from somewhere (whether it had any water was never determined), beautifully polished and manned by firemen in immaculate uniforms and burnished helmets. Another time, in India, the airstrip where they were about to land did not look long enough to Princess Anne who "had made the mistake of accepting the invitation of the captain to view the hills from the cockpit". The exercise was, of course, perfectly safe. Flying during the day in equatorial Africa can be uncomfortable with thermals buffeting the plane. The landing strips are primitive too—one, Princess Anne recalled being

eight thousand feet up in the mountains but with much higher mountains all round so that the aircraft had to be flown in ever-decreasing

224

circles before it could land. If that was not bad enough, I then had to climb into a Land Rover (looking like a green being of average size from outer space and feeling worse) and drive two thousand feet back up the mountain.

On the ground, travel is by the ubiquitous Land Rover. In Bangladesh, where much of the country is a river delta, she travelled mostly by boat, train or just walked. The advantage of Shanks's pony, Princess Anne explained, is that "you have time to see how well kept the houses are on the inside and the efforts the people have made to follow the example of their health visitor".

Another form of travel is by camel. In India, hers was

amenable and ambled off down the road on its well-worn path through the old town of Jaisalmer in Rajasthan . . . [while] the camel next door to me let off a series of the most revolting flatulently bilious noises I have ever heard when asked to rise to its feet. He, she, or it was apparently not pleased about the position of its passenger, somewhere behind its second, or stern hump. The noise only stopped after it was made to kneel down and the passenger moved behind the forward hump.

Donkeys and skinny mules have transported her in Ethiopia; she has ridden an elephant in Nepal, an experience she found "uplifting" (her word).

To see at first hand the results of the Save the Children Fund's projects and the genuine gratitude of workers and patients alike is more than enough reward for all Princess Anne's hard work. Often she is given presents, like some small carving for her children or, as in the case of her visit to one African country, a small pipe. Needless to say, the British press thought it a hashish pipe, which upset the government of the country. In the Gambia, the headman was insistent that she take a large goat as a present. The goat accompanied them for the rest of the day and "then mysteriously disappeared".

The Save the Children Fund receives a great deal of world-wide publicity through Princess Anne's tours of their overseas projects, but the Fund is just as active, and needed, in Britain as abroad but receives less (or no) coverage. Princess Anne accepts that the media is largely responsible for that imbalance:

There is a natural feeling among the public that there is something not quite nice about a civilised country like Britain needing the Fund. Also, the projects here tend to get local rather than national coverage, but that in a way is good because it shows the Fund's important place in the local community.

Princess Anne is of course as dedicated to the work of the Fund at home as to their projects abroad (they also account for about a third of the Fund's income). Those projects she has not visited personally (some many times over) she is certainly familiar with through written reports. All are connected with child welfare, and range from simple playgroups to special schools for children with behavioural difficulties, like the one near Edinburgh. They run holiday homes for deprived children, mobile playbuses to hospital playgroups and more recently, help for the children of travellers' families who often miss out on the benefits of the State's Health and Social Services. Sometimes, Princess Anne is not as free as she would like to visit some of the projects. She has

talked to our workers in Belfast when I've been in Northern Ireland, but the security situation has not so far made it possible for me to visit the actual projects. I very much hope that this will change one day because there is some excellent and interesting work —locally run playgroups for visiting families attached to the courts and prisons, an intermediate treatment centre to give children from this very difficult environment a more positive view of life, and a city farm just outside the town where older children who have been in trouble can work under supervision.

227

The Save the Children Fund is an entirely voluntary organisation relying on funds raised solely from the public. Since she became their president, there is no doubt that Princess Anne has given them an infinitely higher profile, especially since her trips to Third World countries have been so widely reported. In 1971 the income of the Fund was less than £4 million. By 1984 it had risen to £16.5 million with a record £42.5 million in 1985 (the year of the world-wide response to the Ethiopian famine). Obviously these phenomenal increases are not due to Princess Anne alone, but every time she is seen on television in some far-flung corner of the world or at a charity event, the funds do come in faster.

Princess Anne never misses an opportunity to raise money for "her" charity. She takes great pleasure in raising money from unexpected quarters. She extracted a sizeable donation from the delegates she addressed at the meeting of the Inland Revenue Staff Federation. When speaking to a conference of freight hauliers, she spoke of the work of the Save the Children Fund and, not long after, one large courier company agreed to deliver their medicines anywhere in the world, free of charge. Michael Parkinson invited her on to his chat-show in Australia. Princess Anne agreed but only after a donation of £6,000 was sent to the Fund.

Much of her time is spent with other charitable organisations receiving gifts raised for the

Fund. On 12 February 1986 she went to the Bristol Chamber of Commerce to receive a Land Rover for an SCF project in Jamaica. The next day, she received a large cheque from Westminster Christmas Appeal for the children's hospital in Khartoum. She had three engagements in Glasgow on the fifteenth; attended a "Tea Challenge" put on by the Tea Council in London on the seventeenth; then north to Sunderland to visit the Milestone Centre for young offenders. She was back in London on 23 February for a performance of the Messiah at the Royal Albert Hall.

It has even been said that she takes on the patronage of extra organisations, like the British Knitwear and Clothing Export Council, as a means of widening "her net" for support for the Save the Children Fund. Whether an exaggerated claim or no, she still puts in the same amount of hard work to the organisation as any.

Apart from the large-scale balls and film premières in aid of the Save the Children Fund, she attends every other conceivable event that her busy schedule allows, from dolls' house exhibitions to greyhound racing. She likes to involve her family as well in fund-raising. There is the annual clay-pigeon shoot, often won by "The Team" of Mark Phillips, Prince Andrew, the Duke of Kent and King Constantine. Other teams are made up from friends—Jackie Stewart has a team which has Prince Albert of Monaco,

Angus Ogilvy and Anthony Andrews—and sports and show business personalities including Steve Cauthern, Jack Charlton and Suzie Quattro.

Of the future, Princess Anne has said, "It would be nice to say that the Save the Children Fund will never be required, but somehow you know that is never going to be true." So long as the Fund is there, one thing is certain, Princess Anne will be there to steer it forward. In 1982, one severely handicapped boy, Nyasha Mvaimvai, from Zimbabwe wrote a poem for her:

You tree, you are a beautiful thing,
You are the life of everybody,
You give us fruit, shade and the air we
    breathe
Your leaves are beautiful like a bride on her
    wedding day.

The subject, of course, is a tree, but then it could also have been the President of the Save the Children Fund.

10

Princess for the Future

ONE of the great strengths of the Royal Family is its ability to change with the times, yet remain as a symbol of permanence and stability. They are not above seeking the advice of their courtiers or, if they do not have the expertise, experts from outside are brought in. Often, the advice is unsolicited, like that from the public relations consultancy, Neilson McCarthy, through the Prince of Wales's Private Secretary, Squadron Leader Sir David Checketts. The Investiture and the making of the television film *Royal Family* in 1969—dubbed *Corgi and Beth* by the press, were both enormous successes. Between them, the PR men and the courtiers, they had with perfect timing shown what was to become described as "the human face of Royalty". Whether by design or good luck, they had found a means of projecting the Mountbatten-Windsors as Royal superstars in a manner that a television-mad and demanding audience could devour with unending interest.

The old order, naturally, kicked against such a popular image but once such an image was created, there was no going back. Milton Shulman, the theatre critic for the *Evening Standard* asked:

Is it, in the long run, wise for the Queen's advisers to set as a precedent this right of the television camera to act as an image-making apparatus for the monarchy? Every institution that has so far attempted to use TV to popularise or aggrandise itself, has been trivialised by it.

Where Shulman's question was totally valid at the time, judging by hindsight nearly twenty years later, the answer must be in the affirmative. Certainly television, both at home and abroad, has contributed greatly to that successful and popular image of the Royal Family today. Far from trivialising them, television has considerably boosted them. A great measure of that success must be due to Princess Anne herself. It is no accident that she is the member of the Royal Family who is most seen on television or heard on the radio. Her qualities are easily recognisable, and not just to those who are there to foster the Royal image. She is a natural performer, without a trace of nerves, whether real or suppressed. From the very beginning, she has appeared knowledgeable and well-informed. She can speak on any subject and those topics that she does not care to talk about, she ignores

232

with an icy glare or deflects in a skilful manner: "Generally speaking, it would be true to say that there is an argument which says . . ." Above all, she is an "intelligent communicator", her personal conviction on a subject is totally credible. She will not say anything for effect. Mark Bowden who co-ordinates the Save the Children Fund's projects in Africa has said, "The Princess makes up her own mind and comes up with her own advice and suggestions."

Not long after Princess Anne took over the Presidency of the Save the Children Fund, she was invited to appear in the children's television programme, *Blue Peter*, the presenter, Valerie Singleton,

was terribly nervous at first, because I didn't quite know what to expect the Princess would be like. All I was told was that I should call her Ma'am. The first time we filmed with her on the plane, the Princess was terrific. I didn't feel at all nervous after the first interview. No, they weren't interviews really, they were just conversations. She is really marvellous when it comes to making people relax. We filmed every day for eight days with her, and what impressed us most about her was that she is genuinely interested in everything she sees.

She was very co-operative and very quick to grasp what was wanted of her while we were filming. We didn't talk about anything that was personal, but you can gather a lot about someone's character just discussing everyday things.

Princess Anne and Valerie Singleton flew to Kenya and between visiting various Save the Children projects, including the Statehe Boys' School in Nairobi, the two women were seen in the game parks and riding two rather thin horses. When the film, *Blue Peter Royal Safari*, was screened on a Sunday afternoon in 1970 viewers saw first-hand just what a force Princess Anne had become and, even at the age of twenty, she knew what she was talking about. Her previous film, *The Princess and the Children* made by Michael Benson, won various television awards in the social services category but, for some reason, was never screened in Britain.

Since then, a number of films have been made of Princess Anne, mostly in her capacity as president or patron of her two main charities. Like her presence at a fund-raising occasion, her appearance, however short, raises the tone of a film. Films made especially about her work at home and, more recently, her trips abroad, have also helped to demonstrate to the public just how hard she does work. Thames Television made a seventy-five minute documentary on a year of her working life, which was screened as part of ITV's Christmas viewing on 23 December 1981. One of the most revealing insights into Princess

Anne's spartan trips was *Saving the Children*, an account of her tour of the Gambia and Burkino Fasso, shown on Independent TV on her return. She did most of the voice-over of the film but, more important, there was no disguising, nor attempts to disguise, how primitive these places were. Her trips took their rightful place as major news items and were treated as such. David Frost interviewed her for TV-AM before she left for Bangladesh and India, starting with the proposed tour before going on to discuss a wide range of topics.

If these insights into her working life did much to change the public's view of Princess Anne, her guest appearances on various chat shows did more. Apart from the obvious coup to the host and the television company of having a member of the Royal Family on their programme, they do give Princess Anne a chance to put her point of view and correct many inaccuracies that have irked her in the past. It also gave the public a chance to appreciate her fine sense of humour and ready wit—she even held her own when she lunched on 4 March 1975 with the humorous magazine *Punch*, and was granted the great honour of being the first woman to carve her name on the table. It is interesting that she just put part of her initials, AP, on the table instead of "Anne" or "PA" (Princess Anne). Both Michael Parkinson and Terry Wogan enjoyed having her on their shows, both being surprised at how easily the conversation flowed. It was a brave Princess Anne who took on Radio 4's live "phone-in", *Tuesday Call*. Listeners were invited to telephone the BBC which they did, putting a wide range of questions.

The Queen only occasionally appears on film or in a television programme today, although the Duke of Edinburgh often takes part in interviews and films on subjects that interest him, mainly the World Wildlife Fund and carriage driving. Princess Margaret was once a guest on the late Roy Plomley's *Desert Island Discs*, while the only other member of the Royal Family of that generation who is ever-available to the media is Princess Michael of Kent. The Prince and Princess of Wales occasionally let the cameras and interviewers into their private life; the Princess generally let off with carefully scripted questions, while Prince Charles, though sincere in his approach, not exactly sparkling with his excessive references as to how old he has become. In time, more attention will be paid to Prince Andrew and Prince Edward, especially when they abandon their Service careers and mount the public platform. Thus, it is left to Princess Anne, that most articulate of all the Royal communicators, to "front" for the Royal Family—to the public's enjoyment and her gain.

It was a sparkling Princess Anne that exchanged quick, witty repartee with the BBC's presenter, Terry Wogan, on his show on the evening of 20 March 1985, the *badinage* going so well that it almost could have been scripted (which, of course, it was not). Wogan, having led her through various aspects of her life, brought the conversation round to her public image:

"Are you conscious of the fact," he asked her, "that what they call in this business your image has improved over the past few years?"

"Hmm!" Princess Anne replied with a grin, then after a long pause, "You're telling me . . . I like to ask people what they were expecting before they met me, and then I find out what my image was."

Wogan walked straight into her trap. "What do they say when you ask them that?"

To which she replied with the sweetest smile, "I am just about to ask you that!"

After the applause and laughter had died down, Wogan gallantly replied, "Well you see, ma'am, the problem is if I tell you that, it will only make you blush in all modesty!"

A smiling Princess Anne murmured, "Oh . . . well, perhaps you might forget it."

Terry Wogan either deliberately fell into the trap or should have been better briefed by his researchers, for that is her stock reply to the same question, asked many times before. Kenneth Harris in his interview for the *Observer* as long ago as 1980 asked about her newspaper image. Likewise, she turned the question round and asked him if she was what he expected. She would not let him off until he had qualified his "No, very different" with:

Outside your family, you seem to be only interested in horses—eventing. You seem to be impatient, with newspapers generally and with photographers in particular. And you seem not to care very much what impression you create on people.

Had he been speaking for the "popular" press, he could have added dozens of pejorative terms:

From Jean Rook in the *Daily Express* in 1979: "She publicly speaks badly. She publicly relates badly by looking morose on foreign trips. She's bored and shows it, with her job as a Royal and, for a mother, she's lousy at handling other people's kids." *The Sunday People* in 1982 came up with, "Anne would be earning her keep if she learned how to tame her tongue, and suppress her sulks." The *Daily Mail* contrasted Prince Andrew, "handsome and smiling . . . warm and friendly" with her as, "plain and sulky . . . cold and prickly". *The Sun* coined the sobriquet "Her Royal Haughtiness", and described her "arrogance, rudeness and sheer bad temper".

Nor were such criticisms confined to Britain. During her first trip to Australia in 1970 with the Queen, the Duke of Edinburgh and the Prince of Wales, the republicans among them gave her no quarter. Her critics were vociferous; they heckled her at one engagement and told her to "clear off" at a university campus. She ignored them, apparently unperturbed, only to be presented with a bunch of weeds with a mock curtsey. A "river of blood" was spilled at her feet, a symbol of the "lost cause of Royalty". The Norwegians branded her on the front page of their papers as "cold and callous" for sweeping past a small boy in a hospital in Oslo. The retraction of the fabricated story that appeared the next day was lost on the inside pages. Even the Canadians found a group of children who had been waiting in the "cold and snow" were snubbed by a "snobbish" Princess Anne who had time only for "horsey people". To the Americans, who have their own ideas as to how a princess ought to look and behave, Princess Anne "just doesn't measure up". She has been named by one journalist as "the person I would least like to interview". After a visit to the White House in 1970 as a guest of ex-President Nixon, the *Washington Post* dubbed her "the Royal Sourpuss". While the Prince of Wales was fêted and praised, his sister was rapped over the knuckles for being "sullen, ungracious and plain bored". He was "full of pep", while she "acts pooped".

Princess Anne started well enough. As a small child, the press and public could not have enough of those sweet, fair curls, angelic features and blue eyes, and silk party dresses with frilly petticoats. When she left school at the end of the sixties, she was hailed as the spirit of youth with her daring fashions, mod watch and independent spirit. Fashion magazines carried her on their front covers. She could do no wrong. Then the initial Princess euphoria of the press and public began to wane: the honeymoon was over. However, there was a brief respite when she was forgiven everything for choosing a "handsome cavalry officer" as a husband. Then, it was business as usual with that same difficult relationship with the world's press and a poor showing in the Royal popularity poll that lasted for nearly ten more years.

The roots of such antagonism are threefold: Princess Anne herself, unfortunate circumstances beyond her control and the press themselves. The combination of all three, one played off against the other, made for a stormy and combustible relationship. Fuelled by such reports, the public were only too willing to believe what they read.

When the *Sunday Times Magazine* asked about her image in 1985, Princess Anne modified her stock reply:

I didn't match up to the public's idea of a fairy princess in the first place! The Princess of Wales has obviously filled a void in the media's life which I had *not* filled, but I never had any intention of filling it. I had already made a decision that that wasn't me in any way.

Even as a teenager, she had no desire to be admired just for who she was; she needed to do something special and be needed for herself.

"I'm me," she said, "I'm a person, I'm an individual, and I think it's better for everybody that I am me and shouldn't try to pretend to be anything that I am not." In that, she was a pure Mountbatten, bold, forthright and honest. Until he mellowed, the Duke of Edinburgh had a raging relationship with the press. His outbursts were legion: he has turned a hose-pipe on the press; he asked "Which are the monkeys?" to photographers on the Rock of Gibraltar, while he told the people of Dominica that "You have the mosquitoes, we have the Press". To him, the *Daily Express* is "A bloody awful newspaper. It is full of lies, scandal and imagination." Princess Anne followed him as the tide of unpopularity turned against her; she adopted the same provocative stance as her father, legs at an angle, hands behind her back, head tilted to one side with a defiant, challenging look. She once admitted that "There are always people waiting for me to put my foot in it. Just like my father."

She, too, became famous for her outspokeness and for what Prince Philip called "dontopedology"—opening one's mouth and putting

241

one's foot in it. During her tour of the United States, she told an official that she thought having the bald eagle as their national symbol was "rather a bad choice". Once, she came up against a group of anti-field sport protesters at a meet of the Beaufort hunt. After a heated exchange, she asked, "Who's paying you to do this?" to which came the obvious reply, "Well, *we're* paying *you* to do that." Always forthright, she aired her opinions in public and, far from being admired, became fodder for the press. "How can you *demonstrate* for peace?" she asked some students. When launching HMS *Amazon*, she enraged the Women's Liberation movement when she said, "I reckon I found the answer in this piece of information pertaining to the Amazons, those formidable forerunners to the Women's Liberation Movement with whom, incidentally, I have no sympathy. They were, apparently, at their most formidable on horseback."

To some, her honesty can be interpreted as total lack of co-operation. Unlike her grandmother, she has always refused to do "stunts" for the media. The Queen Mother will automatically slow up, or pause, so that photographers can take the best photographs of her. Not so her grand-daughter. Just after her engagement had been announced, one photographer waited for twelve hours in the pouring rain: "I was so wet I looked as if I had fallen into a swimming pool.

242

As the car drew into the gates I stepped forward with the camera. And then, just as she came alongside, she deliberately turned her whole body in the opposite direction so I couldn't get the shot." Of course, she had no idea how long he had been waiting. The Queen Mother will pose with billiard cues in her hand at boys' clubs, no one ever says an unkind word about her (at least until Penelope Mortimer's biography), so much so, that in those "ten years of frost", there were frequent calls for her grand-daughter to try to emulate her more. Her grand-daughter steadfastly refused. Even on her tours for the Save the Children Fund, she refuses to pick up babies simply to make a more emotive picture. At a party for deprived children in Hyde Park in 1979, she refused to hold a Kermit the Frog toy for photographers. "I'm not Mrs. Thatcher," she informed them. Often, the press and photographers do not know what to make of her and her very advanced sense of humour. Was she joking when one reporter said, "It's lovely to see you again, ma'am", to which she replied, "Oh really, why?" She certainly was not joking when she froze one photographer who asked her "to look this way love" with "I'm not your 'love', I'm Your Royal Highness".

Although much of the criticism levelled at Princess Anne could be justified, there was more that was plainly unfortunate. Invariably, it could easily have been logically explained away, had the media been benevolent or kindly disposed. Even now, she will often look sullen or grim, what Auberon Waugh calls her "nasty nip in the air face", but those that know her well know that, like the Queen and Princess Margaret, when she is not actually smiling or animated by talking, she has the kind of face that looks fierce in repose. She is often attacked over her expression on engagements, but, as she says:

You have to keep an intelligent interest in what is going on, and it is difficult, I always think, to take an intelligent interest *and* wear a grin. Male members of Royalty are not expected to meet such high standards and can appear serious or distant in public without being criticised. Men can be serious. They are allowed to be.

Often, Princess Anne is appearing with a more senior member or members of the Royal Family. There she is "tail-end Charlie, rather tail-end Annie" so it would be totally wrong of her to draw attention to herself. In Australia, she was castigated for not being a "being a bundle of joy", but, as she rightly pointed out:

You must understand how difficult it is, when you are fourth in line [the Queen, the Duke of Edinburgh and the Prince of Wales] to look bright and smiling all the time. You can't smile *all* the time. It wasn't that I was feeling dull or even bored. It was simply that I was waiting.

She has had her critics, both in public and in the press, that she simply drove past ignoring the crowd. "She never even looked my way", has been a common complaint, but, as she rightly says in reply, "There is a limit to what your neck can do."

The two definite areas of Princess Anne's life, public and private, never overlap. She will never discuss her family in public (nor they her) and should she be asked, the question is either ignored or a sharp, defensive reply comes back. When asked her reaction to the birth of Prince William, she shrugged off the questions by asking them for more information, then agreeing that too much fuss was being made of the birth. Undeterred, they kept on, asking her how she felt on becoming an aunt, "That's my business, thank you," she snapped. Intolerant, yes, but she was right. It was her business. While she can generally cope with protecting her private life and is more than willing to co-operate on her public life, it is in that grey area between the two where communications have broken down. As she says:

I do draw the line as I think one of the features of modern life is that because your public life

245

is more easily scrutinised than it was in the past, your private life becomes so much more important. When I'm at home, that's private, and I expect it to stay that way.

Unfortunately, the grey area I consider to be private is my competitive horse-riding life, which is done in public, in the public eye, and is, I think, treated by the media in exactly the same way as it would be at an official function. Of course, I don't treat it that way, I can't treat it that way as you behave quite differently under competitive circumstances. That is quite difficult to understand if you've never competed seriously at any level.

The horse has always smacked of privilege, from the days of squires and knights, mounted infantry officers to today's expensive equine pastimes. Nothing arouses greater antipathy, not even equally expensive sports like fast cars, sailing, shooting or fishing, than the horse. It divides the classes, it separates town from country. Newspaper photographers, in the main, are totally urban. They have no conception of a horse's temperament or what the rider is trying to do—exceptions like Tim Graham and Mike Roberts are rare, and thus well respected in their field. The photographers who followed her were after the most dramatic shot possible, the reporters the best story. They had no respect, or understanding of what she was trying to do. So their intrusion into her private world produced such memorable quotes as "Don't you think I've got enough problems without you?" to one photographer at a horse trials in Ayrshire, and "You're getting on my goat. I've just got this horse settled and now you've upset him. How long are you going to keep this up?" to another who had appeared with his motor-drive camera in the collecting ring before her dressage test, and the most famous remark of all, "Why don't you naff off, go on, shove off!"

Naff has now become common usage, even included in the new *Slang and Unconventional English*. The dictionary notes that it was "alleged to have been said to an importunate press man by Princess Anne at Badminton Horse Trials, 1982"—and of being a mid-nineteenth-century term for "ffuck". She told two *Daily Mirror* photographers to "piss off" at the Crondall Horse Trials, Hampshire, later that same year. Such behaviour upset both parties but, for certain sections of the press, it did make for a better story. Once they knew how she would react, some went so far as to goad her into losing her temper. She puts the choice of words down to either the Buckingham Palace Girl Guides or school. "That's school, not Palace or even horsey circles, I learned to swear at Benenden."

Sometimes, the blame could have been laid with her. There was one account the day before the European Championships at Burghley when two photographers were waiting when she turned up at the stableyard. According to one of them, she was looking "quite stunning . . . wearing brightly coloured slacks, a red, white and blue sweater and had her hair down". One of them said, "Sorry, Ma'am, but if we can get a picture of you now, we'll be off. We don't want to be pests." It was a perfectly polite and reasonable request but the subject rounded on him with "You *are* pests, by the very nature of the camera in your hands". There are two sides to every story but Princess Anne was always the loser—the cards are stacked against her.

Once she was out of favour with the media, Princess Anne could do nothing right. Here, certain sections of the press were certainly guilty of an appalling bias. Where she went about her public engagements with true professionalism and dedication, they were invariably reported with enthusiasm by the local press. When these same visits made the national press, they were often misreported. The child that was missed in the crowd outside made better copy than the hundreds she met and charmed inside. On her public engagements, she barely notices the press.

On a day out or at an engagement, they are part of the scenery. Obviously there are places where they get in the way more, and that doesn't so much affect me as it affects the people at that particular engagement, be it, for instance, at the Riding for the Disabled groups where one tends to worry a little bit because most of the ponies don't see large numbers of people, and they certainly don't see flashlights and cameras, so that is a problem, and I'm always ready to have words in their shell-like ears about minding their manners because they don't notice to a large extent what they're doing and the effect they're having. But equally there are places where they simply get in the way—not of me but of other people, but that's part of a working day.

The battle between the Royal Family and the media has been raging on and off for centuries. "Today [16 October 1982]" the *Spectator* wryly pointed out, "the 'public's right to know' is circumscribed only by the capacity of security men to stop photographers climbing into bedrooms."

It was not quite as bad in the last century, but even Queen Victoria complained about their intrusion into her private life in her journal, during 1873:

About ten miles from Ballachulish . . . we sat down on the grass (we three) on our plaids, and had our luncheon, served by Brown and Francie, and then I sketched. The day was most beautiful and calm. Here, however—

here in this complete solitude, we were spied upon by impudent, inquisitive reporters, who followed us everywhere; but one in particular (who writes for some of the Scottish papers) lay down and watched with a telescope and dogged me and Beatrice [her daughter] and Jane Churchill, who were walking about, and was most impertinent when Brown told him to move, which Jane herself had thought of doing. However, he did go away at last, and Brown came back saying he thought there would have been a fight; for when Brown said, quite civilly, that the Queen wishes him to move away, he said that he had quite as good a right to remain there as the Queen. To this Brown answered very strongly, upon which the impertinent individual asked, "Did he know who he was?" and Brown answered that he did, and that "the highest gentleman in England would not dare do what he did, much less a reporter—and he must move on, or he would give him something more". And the man said, "Would he dare do that before those other men (all reporters) who were coming up?" And Brown answered, "Yes" he would before "anybody who did not behave as he thought fit". More strong words were used; but the others came up and advised the man to come away quietly, which he finally did.

Such conduct ought to be known.

Since the reign of George III, notification of the Royal family and their movements have appeared in the Court Circular, and it was he, "annoyed by the inaccuracies in the papers as to the Royal movements, took the advice of the Chief Metropolitan Magistrate and appointed a Court Newsman". Today, the Press Office at Buckingham Palace, under the Queen's press secretary, Michael Shea, liaises between the Royal Family and the press. Michael Shea has two assistant press secretaries, Victor Chapman (known by the press as "Rowdy Yates" after the television cowboy from *Rawhide* whose stock phrase is "round 'em up and move 'em out") and John Haslam, who also handles Princess Anne's press affairs. It is they who spend much of their time either persuading newsmen to leave the family in peace, or denying the more outrageous stories.

Such stories are so ludicrous that they are amusing. The European press is famous for its inventive powers: Princess Anne asked the editor of *Paris Match*, "Am I divorced yet?" shortly after her wedding. In 1972 *France Dimanche* analysed its cuttings on the Royal Family to find that over the previous fourteen years they had reported that the Queen was about to abdicate sixty-three times, divorce on seventy-three separate occasions, fallen out with Lord Snowdon 115 times and Princess Grace of Monaco seventeen times, and been pregnant

251

ninety-two times—only on two occasions were they correct. The supposed break-up of Princess Anne's marriage appeared in *Jours de France*: "Anne et Mark Phillips: de Nouveau Nuages", but they made nothing of the resignation of Cecil Parkinson and the scandal that surrounded it.

Princess Margaret and Princess Anne have shared the brunt of fabricated stories, especially over the state of their marriages. Stories of rifts between "Anne and Mark" became monotonous in their regularity. Every year when Princess Anne went to Balmoral in the late summer without her husband, the same story appeared. The fact that the holiday coincided with the harvest was never considered. That they stayed in separate hotels in Los Angeles for the 1984 Olympics, was taken as yet another rift—Princess Anne was there as the President of the British Olympic Association, Mark Phillips went as a commentator for an Australian television network. Both stayed in their own "camps". If that was not enough, the media made much out of Daly Thompson's remark at his press conference. When asked what Princess Anne had said to him after he had won his decathlon gold medal, he replied, "She said I was a damn good looking guy"—his way of telling the press that it was nothing to do with them what she had said. At least Princess Anne saw the joke.

Family feuds are popular too. Much was made of the fact that Princess Anne did not attend the christening of Prince Harry but, as she explained, but no one wanted to listen, they really did have a long-standing prior engagement. Her children went, and more than made up for their parents with their decibels. After so long, such reports really do not worry Princess Anne: "If it is completely untrue, then it doesn't hurt at all because, in a way, it doesn't matter."

Throughout her life, the media have shown varying amounts of interest in her and her development. Some reports are accurate, some idiotic, some unnecessary. A staff reporter in his wisdom informed the readers of the *Daily Telegraph* that Princess Anne had heard a sermon during her first term at Benenden on the theme that "There is an obsession with sex. You cannot read or hear anything, or go to the cinema without it being brought in. Forget it. It is only a trifle". Was it necessary for the *Spectator* to publish an article asking "Has Princess Anne had sex?" under the title *Princess Anne and the Facts of Life?* The predictable storm followed and the literary editor, Maurice Cowling, resigned when the *Spectator* refused to "print a critical letter from him and failed to express regret for the article".

If the media had tarnished Princess Anne's image, it was they who polished it and restored her to her rightful position. The renaissance of her popularity has been set at the end of 1982. She admitted in 1985 that the sort of image that you get is seldom of your own doing . . . I have a suspicion—I don't quite know why—but when I went on a rather longer trip to Africa, quite a number of press who came I think were looking for trouble. I don't think they had any idea of what sort of trips I did, and thought that it would be right for trouble-making, or just that I was about to make a nonsense of it. When they actually saw the sort of trips I did it possibly changed their attitude to the sort of things I did.

The trouble that Princess Anne referred to in this case was yet another "rift in her marriage".

Even she noticed her "miraculous transformation", as she put it, in the press, although she adamantly denies that it is she who has changed. "The media", she concedes, "are just showing me in a different light." It is much more likely that it is a combination of the two: the media recognises her for her true worth, and she has mellowed.

The *volte face* of the media, however, was immediate. For example, Jean Rook, who had been so jaundiced about her before, wrote in 1984 that "she had proved herself to be a magnificent, courageous young woman. She'd make a hell of a latter-day Nightingale, Curie, Queen Victoria or member of the SAS". The transformation in her media coverage has also been, so far, permanent. Listeners to the *Today* programme on Radio 4 voted her the runner up as the "Woman of the Year" in 1985 but she came out top in 1986, polling more votes than all the other candidates put together. Princess Anne could do no wrong. Suddenly, the person that the media and the public had all "learned" to dislike, became a heroine. "Her Royal Helpfulness" replaced the "Royal Haughtiness" tag of old.

It would be too easy to put the "miracle" transformation down to the recognition of just one tour, however arduous, uncomfortable or effective it was. Some would have it that not seeing her continually on a horse made her critics take her more seriously; they began to realise just how much she had actually achieved. But the whole of the image of the Royal Family is changing—it has to change with the times in order to survive. Malcolm Muggeridge coined the expression that they were the "Royal Soap Opera" as long ago as 1955, but the Royal Family are more real, entertaining with far higher audience ratings than any canned series of the mega-rich from the United States. The older members of the cast, although still very much in evidence, are now not quite so prominent. The much-loved Queen Mother is in her late eighties, marching alongside the years of the century; the Queen, who still increases her work-load, stands for the old order; likewise the Duke of Edinburgh who works quietly away with his specialised public engagements and his presidency of the World Wildlife Fund, but without his former, outspoken brio. The new star to the performance is, of course, the Princess of Wales, riding high on her popularity by dint of her beauty, freshness and genuine, caring approach. But Princess Anne had thirteen years start on her in the public eye. While recognising the Princess of Wales's great contribution to the "family firm", Princess Anne dismisses totally, and rightly, that the recognition of her work had anything to do with whom her brother had married. The Princess of Wales's husband has been very carefully stage-managed. In his early years, he was groomed for stardom but, before he could put a foot wrong, he scuttled back into the Royal Navy. By the time he had emerged again, Princess Anne had already made her mark, favourable to those who recognised her talents, black to the media and her unsympathetic public.

Possibly, such a black image has been to her advantage—it is best to know the worst before you can appreciate the best. The undoubted disparity between the image and reality has finally been realized. Some say that there was a directive from the Queen herself for parity for her daughter. Such a suggestion is strongly denied by her press secretary, John Haslam: "If there was any decision, it came from Princess Anne herself." Wherever the incentive came from, whatever the result, Princess Anne is the force to carry the Royal Family forward to the twenty-first century.

THE END

Other titles in the
Charnwood Library Series:

THE MAYOR OF CASTERBRIDGE
by Thomas Hardy

Michael Henchard whilst drunk sells his wife and child in a fairground auction. Returning to his senses he takes a solemn vow not to touch intoxicants for twenty years. By his energy he becomes rich, respected, and the Mayor of Casterbridge (Dorchester), but his past rises up and destroys him. The story of a personal tragedy—of the rise and fall of a single man, undone by his faults of character and the changing conditions of rural commerce. His struggles against his society and his own guilty past have a truly heroic grandeur.

THE HIDDEN TARGET
by Helen MacInnes

Student terrorists mysteriously financed, senior secret agency officials setting up Interintell to counter the international threat, and caught between them Nina O'Connell, studying art in London, shut out of her father's life by his new marriage and his busy Washington career. Nina impulsively joins a group to drive around the world in a custom-built caravan, undeterred by the warnings of the attractive Nato officer who once helped a susceptible school girl to improve her tennis game, and finds herself inextricably mixed up in international terrorism.

NEVER LEAVE ME
by Harold Robbins

The author has previously written of the ugly, seamy side of New York, here he shows that the oak-panelled offices of big business, and expense account frolics of Madison Avenue hucksters, are not very far removed from this jungle world. Life in New York's upper income brackets is just as vicious, cruel and deadly as life on the lower East Side. The story of one man—one of that select group who build dreams, create stars and destroy people—and how he almost tore his life to pieces in a frenzy of passion and a hunger for power.

LORD JIM
by Joseph Conrad

Born of Polish parents in the Ukraine, the author went to sea on a French vessel in 1874. In 1878 he joined an English merchant ship, and in 1884 gained his Master's ticket and was naturalised as a British subject. The sea provides a setting for most of his works. His earlier novels reveal him struggling with the difficulties of an unfamiliar language, but he achieved success with this tale, set in eastern waters, of a young Englishman who, in a moment of panic, deserts his apparently sinking ship, loses his honour, and finally retrieves it by an honourable death.

THE GO-BETWEEN
by L. P. Hartley

The hero of this novel is a boy of twelve, with a propensity for day-dreaming. In the summer of 1900 he pays a visit to a schoolfriend at a Norfolk country house, and there becomes involved in a drama between three grown-up people which brings tragedy to one of them and to the boy himself, temporary loss of memory and a lasting distrust of life. Fifty years later the chance discovery of some relics dating from those days recalls the visit, and, trying to remember it, he tells the story.

JANE EYRE
by Charlotte Brontë

This novel was first published in October 1847. The author's first novel, *The Professor*, had been rejected and Charlotte concluded that the publishers preferred the "wild, wonderful and thrilling" to the "plain and homely". *Jane Eyre* certainly contains elements of the "thrilling" which recall the Gothic novels. Its originality lay partly in the choice of a small, plain, governess as its heroine: partly in the skilful manipulation of the first person narrative. Jane's childhood experiences evoke sympathy and part of the fascination of the novel's later progress is the convergence of the developing and mature character of Jane.

TRIPLE
by Ken Follett

A novel of espionage and intrigue. Israeli Intelligence learns that Egypt is building a nuclear reactor. To survive, Israel must negate the plan and build her own, but how to get hold of the vital uranium? Nat Dickstein, hero of Israel—The Pirate—is asked by Mossad to mastermind the most daring feat of piracy for his country. He must face too his love for a half-English, half-Arab girl, for where does her allegiance lie? And, breathing down his neck, is the ruthless K.G.B. agent Rostov and a bitter, stateless Yassif recruited to Egyptian Intelligence.

SHIBUMI
by Trevanian

In this novel of action and suspense set against a background of Europe and Japan, the author, master of the anti-hero, has created in Nicholai Hel a warrior-philosopher, the perfect assassin for our times. A brutal C.I.A. spoiling raid has left nine shattered, bloody bodies lying in Rome Airport. A woman, Hannah Stern, has escaped. Both the C.I.A. and its sinister "Mother Company" are determined to track Hannah down and eliminate her. The chase leads to Hel, an almost legendary killer who has served most of the world's paymasters.

THE SCARLATTI INHERITANCE
by Robert Ludlum

The Third Reich is in its death struggle. In Washington word is received that an elite member of the Nazi High Command is willing to defect and divulge information that will shorten the war. But his defection entails the release of the ultra-top-secret file on the Scarlatti Inheritance—a file whose contents will destroy many of the Western world's greatest and most illustrious reputations if they are made known . . . A story of international terror and intrigue, greed and cunning, suspense and murder.

McINDOE'S ARMY
by Peter Williams and Ted Harrison

The badly injured airmen of World War II who were treated by the eminent plastic surgeon Sir Archibald McIndoe and his team at East Grinstead formed a Club, The Guinea-Pig Club. Many had suffered severe burns to face and hands, but thrived in the atmosphere of humour and comradeship which McIndoe created. The Club survives and thrives today, providing company, encouragement and practical help for its members. But what of the future? Its members grow older. Will the knowledge they've gained die with them? How should the Club pass on its experience of the problems burn victims face?

A PASSAGE TO INDIA
by E. M. Forster

First published in 1924, a novel "out-of-time"—neither precisely pre-war nor precisely post-war, and deliberately free from direct political reference. Dominated by the theme of barriers between individuals of the same or of different races in India under the British Raj, it is perhaps the most impressive novel by any European about Asia. A novel in which England said goodbye for ever to Kipling's simplified views of Anglo-India and where a liberal mind saw the tragic irony, as well as the incidental humour, of the lack of contact between East and West.

THE OFFICER'S WOMAN
by Margot Arnold

This romantic and robust novel of nineteenth century England unfolds the story of Elizabeth, seeing through her eyes the people who influenced her life on the fringes of Society: her friends like the astute little lawyer Jeremy Winter who never lost his exasperated affection for her; her lovers—the domineering Colonel Carter, the depraved Captain Charteris, and Sir Henry Rushden, elderly and kindly. And, moving gradually into the foreground of the story, the man who might give her the happiness she never expected, and dared not hope for.

NINETEEN EIGHTY-FOUR
by George Orwell

A nightmare story of an authoritarian state of the future and of one man's hopeless struggle against it and final defeat by acceptance. Winston Smith, the hero, has no heroic qualities, only a wistful longing for truth and decency. But in a social system where there is no privacy and to have unorthodox ideas incurs the death penalty, he knows that there is no hope for him. His brief love affair ends in arrest by the Thought Police, and when, after months of torture and brain-washing, he is released, he makes his final submission of his own accord.

THE CLOWNS OF GOD
by Morris West

Pope Gregory XVII has done much to give the Vatican a voice that is listened to both among the peoples of the world, and by leading Governments. But suddenly he abdicates his office. The world press is informed that he is in ill health, but the facts are different. The Vatican cardinals have given the Pontiff an ultimatum: "Go, or we will have you certified insane". The reason? Gregory XVII claims to have received a revelation of the end of the world and the Second Coming of Christ. He also believes that he must proclaim this revelation in an encyclical letter to the Church.

THE NAKED ISLAND
by Russell Braddon

The Naked Island has been acclaimed as a classic of World War II. Employing understatement and fierce humour alternatively, Russell Braddon describes the disastrous Malayan campaign of 1942 and the long captivity that followed it. For almost four years his Japanese captors—believing that only death could redeem those who had "dishonourably" surrendered—subjected their 40,000 prisoners to a pitiless regime of starvation and slavery. Theirs, however, was not a code to which the author and his comrades were prepared to subscribe. Instead, drawing upon unsuspected resources of hatred, humour and defiance, they battled to survive.

NORTH AND SOUTH
by Mrs. Gaskell

Quite a group of novelists in the forties and fifties of the last century used their work as a medium for setting forth, in no uncertain voice, the sufferings of the poor. The author took her place as a staunch defender of the distressed Lancashire operatives by her first novel *Mary Barton*. *North and South*, which the author once admitted was her favourite story, and described as one of the finest novels of modern English fiction, is a north country story of daily life in a manufacturing district.

KENILWORTH
by Sir Walter Scott

The story is based on the tradition of the tragic fate, in the reign of Queen Elizabeth, of the beautiful Amy Robsart, daughter of Sir Hugh Robsart of Devon. Beguiled by her charms, the Earl of Leicester, the Queen's favourite, has secretly married her and established her at Cumnor Place. Caught in a net of ambition and intrigue Leicester is forced to acknowledge that Amy is his wife, thereby calling down on himself the furious anger of the jealous Queen. A sycophant, Richard Varney, convinces Leicester that Amy is guilty of infidelity, and in a passion Leicester orders her death.

CAPTAINS COURAGEOUS
by Rudyard Kipling

The story of how an accident changes the character of a rich, spoilt boy called Harvey Cheyne. Swept overboard from a liner bound for Europe, he is picked up by a trawler and forced to work hard to earn his keep. The skipper, Disko Troop, refuses to turn his boat around and land Harvey, so it is nearly a year later when he is reunited with his parents. His father, an American millionaire, is pleased to find that this "unsatisfied dough-faced youth" has become a respectful, and healthy young man.